Bonding over Beauty

A MOTHER-DAUGHTER BEAUTY GUIDE TO FOSTER SELF-ESTEEM, CONFIDENCE, AND TRUST

Erika Katz

GREENLEAF
BOOK GROUP PRESS

This book is intended as a reference volume only, not as a medical manual. The information given here is designed specifically to help mothers of young daughters make informed decisions about health issues concerning them. It is not intended as a substitute for any treatment that may have been prescribed by a doctor. If you suspect that your child has a medical problem, you should seek competent medical help. You should not begin a new health regimen without first consulting a medical professional.

Published by Greenleaf Book Group Press
Austin, Texas
www.gbgpress.com

Distributed by Greenleaf Book Group LLC

For ordering information or special discounts for bulk purchases, please contact Greenleaf Book Group LLC at PO Box 91869, Austin, TX 78709, 512.891.6100.

Design and composition by Greenleaf Book Group LLC
Cover design by Greenleaf Book Group LLC
Cover and interior illustrations by Ted Dawson

Publisher's Cataloging-In-Publication Data (Prepared by The Donohue Group, Inc.)
Katz, Erika.
    Bonding over beauty : a mother-daughter beauty guide to foster self-esteem, confidence, and trust / Erika Katz.—1st ed.
        p. : col. ill. ; cm.
    ISBN: 978-1-60832-098-1
    1. Mothers and daughters. 2. Girls—Health and hygiene. 3. Women—Health and hygiene. 4. Beauty, Personal—Psychological aspects. I. Title.
HQ755.85 .K38 2011
306.874/3   2010937579

Part of the Tree Neutral® program, which offsets the number of trees consumed in the production and printing of this book by taking proactive steps, such as planting trees in direct proportion to the number of trees used: www.treeneutral.com

Printed in the United States of America on acid-free paper

11 12 13 14 15   10 9 8 7 6 5 4 3 2 1

First Edition

This book is dedicated to mothers and daughters everywhere.

Foreword

Say mother-daughter relationship and immediately you usher in a host of beliefs, expectations, notions, and myths surrounding how that relationship is supposed to be. Each and every daughter wants her mom to be loving, accepting, nurturing, supportive, understanding, and trustworthy. Each wants a mom who she can turn to, who she can share her problems and secrets with, and who will make it all better and make her feel safe again. Each little girl wants to look up to her mom, respect her, and believe in her as a role model. She wants somebody with whom she can identify and who will help her gain the confidence she needs to grow into a secure young woman.

How hard should it be for a mother to love her daughter and accept, listen to, support, and understand her daughter's needs and feelings? It should not be that difficult to be that friend she can count on when the challenges of growing up seem so overwhelming.

Yet, mother-daughter relationships are far from simple. They are conflicted, difficult, and for so many, a tremendous source of disappointment, riddled with misunderstanding and resentment.

Often, mothers try to "help" and take care of their daughters by "telling" them what to do. After all . . . mother knows best. What typically follows is all down hill. The well-intentioned help is perceived as control and criticism by daughters. Rather than moms being able to share what they know in a supportive and helpful way, mother-daughter interactions often turn into giant power struggles, with each feeling rejected by the other.

Additionally, some moms, despite their best intentions, end up missing in action because they are simply too busy and overloaded in their lives to pay the close attention often needed to steer their daughters in the right direction. And finally, some moms, due to cultural differences, simply do not know how to relate to their daughters or be empathetic to what they are experiencing.

So what's a mom to do? How can we find the road into our daughters' hearts? How do we give them the guidance and advice so desperately needed in a way that will be welcomed and appreciated?

Here's exactly where *Bonding over Beauty* by Erika Katz comes to the rescue!

Erika knows first hand how hard it is to be a mom and how difficult it is to be a daughter left to your own devices. She was a young child actress who had to grow up fast. Surrounded by grown ups who assumed she "knew" what to do as a young girl, she was forced to fend for herself. But adolescence is punctuated by land mines and any one can explode and leave you facing an embarrassing, humiliating, and shameful situation. If this happens, it can become a "freeze frame" in time that can reverberate and plague a girl for a lifetime. In fact, that's what happened to Erika when she got her period. She got it publicly, during a photo shoot with everyone's eyes on her—and she was wearing a leotard. Nobody had told her what to expect, nobody had explained what a period was, and so she was completely blindsided.

This devastating experience fueled her desire to protect and prevent other young girls from going through what she did. This passion led her to write a book for girls explaining everything they needed to know that she believed could make or break a childhood, in case their moms didn't tell them.

But then Erika had an "Aha!" moment: it's not the daughters but the moms who need to know—what to say, what to do, and most significantly, how to bond with their daughters so they can create and share the positive, loving, supportive relationship each wants. As a trained psychotherapist, I talk to mothers and daughters all the time. I also talk about sex on my "Let's Talk Sex" radio show. I find many of the issues girls face in the tween years are much like the topic of sex: most people don't talk about it because they do not know how to and/or are uncomfortable doing so. If mothers had the jargon, the language, and the tips for talking about hair problems and skin problems and all of the changes that happen to a girl's body as she starts to grow up, they might be able to dramatically change the landscape of the relationships they have with their daughters. In *Bonding over Beauty,* they will find the bonding steps that will make talking about growing into a woman and all that comes with it easier. This is a head to toe book that addresses everything that moms tend to think happens naturally and therefore, doesn't get discussed.

Bonding over Beauty will equip moms with the information they need to be truly caring—rather than controlling—with their girls. It will enable moms to educate and empower their daughters to make positive choices. Their daughters will be prepared, confident, and secure as they navigate adolescence. While on the surface this looks like a book about skin deep beauty, it is actually about moms being able to teach their daughters the most important lesson of all: beauty truly comes from within.

Making room to spend quality time with your daughter, even as little as five to ten minutes a day, to share specific tips on the how-tos of growing up in a fun and open-minded way will translate into the self-worth and self-esteem that she will take through life. Mothers can shine the light of love on their daughters and create a rewarding, fulfilling, and truly unique relationship with them. *Bonding over Beauty* will help moms nurture their daughters into women they will feel proud of and who will be equally proud of them. And that's a win-win for everyone.

—Dr. Jane Greer, psychotherapist and author of *What About Me?*
  Stop Selfishness From Ruining Your Relationship; host of the
  "Doctor On Call" radio show at Healthylife.net

Acknowledgments

I would like to thank my daughter, Somer, and my son, Stone, for giving me creative ideas for moms to better bond with their daughters. Without your excitement for the project, I never would have been able to do it. You are the best coauthors I ever could have hoped for. To my husband, Jay, who has given me his unwavering support throughout my endeavor and helped me through each step of the process. Your love has been my strength. I would like to thank my father and brother for being my proofreaders and my biggest cheerleaders. To my mother, for bonding with me over beauty ever since I was a little girl. You instilled self-confidence in me that I carry to this day.

I had so much help in writing this book from so many wonderful experts: John Barrett, Ellin LaVar, Nicolie McNeil, Mario Badescu Salon, Ilona Taithy, Dr. Friedman-Kien, Laura Geller, Maria Maio, Dr. Scott R. Lurie, Cindy Barshop, Lucy Peters, Dr. Edmund Kaplan, Rafael Masiewicz, Kim Nicole Hochstadt, and all the hardworking energetic folks at Greenleaf Book Group.

To Thomas Harrison, whose encouragement and book, *Instinct*, changed my life.

I would also like to thank my dearest friends from childhood who have been my guinea pigs since high school, letting me give them facials while I was in beauty school and trying all my different products while I researched this book. Philice, you were game for anything, giving me carte blanche to do your makeup for yearbook pictures and even on prom night. Melissa, and Dana, you always gave me your complete and utter faith that I could solve all your beauty dilemmas. Liz Lewis, you always told me I was capable of anything and you held my hand every step of the way as I wrote this book.

I would especially like to thank *Seventeen* magazine for giving me an internship during my senior year of high school. There I learned how to develop, research, and write beauty articles—skills I still use today.

There are always people in one's life who tell them the truth because they love them unconditionally and will never let them get away with doing less than their best. I have been fortunate to have special people like that around me who have taught me to feel love and empathy for others. That empathy has helped me to be a better mother and learn to really listen to my children's concerns no matter how trite they may seem to the grown-up world.

This book is the culmination of many things I have done in my life. I am grateful for the opportunity to share it with others.

Contents

Build a Bond That Will Last a Lifetime

When your daughter was born, a bundle of hopes and dreams was placed in your arms. But then you had to figure out how to take care of that bundle. Changing her diaper or nursing your baby girl wasn't a walk in the park, but nothing could prepare you for all the issues that come with a daughter entering her preteen and teen years. By age nine, that sweet little girl is looking in the mirror and wondering if she's fat, stuffing her shirt to see how she will look with breasts, experimenting with makeup, and telling you exactly how she wants to wear her hair each day. These behaviors often start as early as age six. Most moms pass them off as play until their daughters start demanding mirrors in their bedroom, their own makeup, and private time in the bathroom. As a mother of a tween or teen, the most difficult challenge you face is guiding your daughter into womanhood while keeping her an innocent child as long as possible. This is where the drama begins.

As your daughter grows up, the most important aspect of your relationship with her will be trust—the trust you have and show in her and the trust she has in you. The best way to build her trust during the delicate preteen and early teen years is to let her know you understand what she is experiencing and that it is as important to you as it is to her. Often, the divide occurs when her idea of how she should look collides with your sense of aesthetic. As a mom, it's often hard to know how much information to give your daughter and when to give it. But preadolescent and adolescent girls are very self-aware, a fact that many moms resist acknowledging. She might want to shave her legs long before you think she should. Or wear makeup and nail polish to school. Or even streak her hair. How you deal with these issues will be a factor that determines the nature of your relationship going forward. This is your golden opportunity to gain her confidence. Now will determine whether you "get her" or whether you are the "Mom who just doesn't understand."

I began my website, www.bondingoverbeauty.com, to share ideas with moms about hair, skin, makeup, hair removal, nails, healthy eating, puberty, and every other beauty issue under the sun. I wanted moms like me to feel they had all of the information they needed to help their daughters navigate the trials of entering womanhood. As I began my research, I realized that a book you could flip through, depending on the issue of the moment, could be a really helpful reference for moms. I also wanted other moms to see how putting on makeup and experimenting with beauty products could be for their tween what baking brownies was to her when she was a preschooler—simply a way to bond and have fun.

My goal with *Bonding over Beauty* is to dispel myths you may believe because your mom or another important woman in your life told you they were true. For instance, my best friend's mom used to always tell us a lady does not shave her legs above the knee. My grandmother said I should brush my hair one hundred times a day to make it shiny. My favorite myth of all is that virgins can't use tampons. I want you to have all of the *right* information so you can help your daughter discover her natural beauty and give her guidance with things that are not so beautiful, such as body odor, facial hair, and breakouts, among others.

As you will see, I do not hold back my opinions, especially on subjects many women might find objectionable, either because they are set in their ways and thus sensitive to being questioned or they are too embarrassed to talk about puberty, sex, etc. You may not agree with my suggestions, but that's okay; my purpose is to get you thinking about the dilemmas I present. I want every mom to put her daughter's self-esteem front and center, even if it means reevaluating the beliefs she herself holds. For example, if you think girls should not shave their legs until they are thirteen years old, yet your ten-year-old daughter is embarrassed by dark hair on her legs, maybe it's time to rethink your position.

Most of the information in this book is practical and fun. Each chapter has great activities you can do with your daughter to spend time with her and open a healthy dialogue. I use beauty as a vehicle to get the ball rolling. Taking the time to soak your daughter's sweet little feet and giving her a pedicure is a fun way to lavish attention on her while also providing her with the opportunity to talk about what's on her mind.

As a child actress and model, I grew up in the world of beauty and fashion. When I was eleven years old, shooting a Danskin ad, the stylist pulled me off the set because I had just gotten my first period and there was blood all over the leotard and tights. I was mortified. The most horrifying part of the experience was that my mother had never explained menstruation to me. After getting over the initial trauma and learning more about it, I eventually asked my mom about tampons. She told me virgins could not use them because that is what her mother told her. After doing a little research, I discovered that was a myth. I had my pediatrician show me how to use them, and then I taught all of my friends.

After that experience, it was difficult for me to turn to my mother for that kind of advice. It really wasn't her fault; she didn't have the correct information. Now I am the mother of a young girl, and I do not have all the answers either. But I want her to come to me instead of her friends when she has questions or concerns. *Bonding over Beauty* will give you the answers you need to be your daughter's greatest resource for her beauty and hygiene issues. When you have the answers to her questions, you will gain her trust and confidence.

As I was blogging and writing this book, many of my friends confided to me that they did not always know what to say when their daughters came to them with beauty and hygiene questions. Often, they would give their daughters little or no information because they did not have it, what they "knew" was wrong, or they did not believe their daughters were ready for the answers. For example, my friend's daughter had hair on her upper lip and the boys at school were teasing her. She didn't want to go through the pain of waxing, so I suggested to her mom that the girl could shave. "No way!" she said. "It will come back thick like a man's beard." But like many old wives' tales, that's not true. So there was a perfectly simple solution that my friend hadn't even considered because she had been misinformed.

My goal in writing this book was also to facilitate open and honest communication between you and your daughter. If you are there for her when she wants to tweeze her eyebrows, color her hair, or use tampons, she may come to you later when she has a question about sex, drugs, and alcohol. I am all about promoting a strong dialogue to last a lifetime.

If you are uncomfortable talking about her changing body, you need to ask yourself why. This is your chance to have a great relationship with your daughter as she moves into her teen years. Instead of judging her for wanting to shave, show her how to do it and make a girls' day of it. If she wants to wear makeup, instead of just saying no, try to find a middle ground. Rather than lipstick, buy her a lip gloss. She will think you really understand her need to feel beautiful and you will feel she still looks like a child. A simple compromise like that could be the difference between a close relationship and a strained one. Frankly, she is probably going to wear the lip gloss anyway; it's better she put it on in front of you than use her friends' makeup in the bathroom at school.

The great hopes you had for your baby and your little girl needn't disappear in the "dreaded" tween and teen years. This period in her life and yours doesn't have to be a tortured existence of drama and tantrums. In *Bonding over Beauty* I have included everything you need to know to teach your daughter about grooming, hygiene, and her changing body in a way that is in sync with what she wants and needs from you. Reading this book can help you enjoy this time of her life and form a bond of love and trust that will last a lifetime.

CHAPTER 1

Bonding over Her Hair

Hair is a huge part of every girl's life. When a young girl feels her hair looks good, she is more confident. She may go to school feeling more attractive, giving her the ability to concentrate *better* on her schoolwork and relationships and *less* on her appearance. Did you ever think hair could be so powerful? Think about how you feel after you have just had your hair cut and blow-dried. Everything from your complexion to your smile looks and feels better. When you think you look good, it improves your mood and how you feel about yourself.

When it comes to the tween years, it's likely your daughter's idea of great-looking hair will differ from yours. Celebrity stylist John Barrett, of the John Barrett salon at Bergdorf Goodman in New York, and Ellin LaVar, who specializes in ethnic and multi-textured hair and has done the locks of Oprah and Naomi Campbell, are just two of the many experts who have shared some wonderful ideas to help you and your daughter get on the same page when it comes to her hair. In this chapter, you will find the basic information you need to find a happy medium between her need to be stylish and your desire for her to look neat and presentable. You will learn how to handle all hair types, what hair care tools and products you need, and step-by-step instructions to apply hair color. Additionally, I've shared with you the secrets to finding a great salon to meet all of your hair care needs.

One of the toughest hair challenges I have faced is caring for my daughter's hair, which is totally different from mine. It was hard enough to figure out what to do with my own hair. My friends with children of mixed race are often faced with this dilemma as well. The best thing you can do for your daughter is to educate yourself about her hair type and the best tools and products for her. When your daughter thinks you know what you're talking about, she'll trust you when you tell her she looks great. After she sees how great you make her look, she'll trust your advice even more, and you might just have some leverage later on when she wants to shave one side of her head.

Another big issue I continue to face is that my idea of pretty often conflicts with my daughter's idea of *fabulous*. After all, in her mind, she knows what's cool and I do not! So we agree she can wear her hair the way she likes it as long as she keeps it clean and healthy. John Barrett suggests you involve your daughter in deciding how *your* hair should look. Tell her you love her style and take her with you to the hair salon. She may have some great ideas to update your look. When your stylist finishes your hair, suggest your daughter get a haircut too. If you listen to her ideas, she might just listen to yours.

But what do you do if your daughter wants something you feel is completely inappropriate, like dying her hair pink? She may be seeking attention or her rebellion could be starting early. There could even be a larger issue that needs to be addressed. To get the dialogue going, I suggest you start by doing something simple together. As you will find in all the chapters, there are some wonderful mother-daughter activities listed at the end of this chapter that will give you time to talk while doing something fun together.

If she seems unresponsive, you could take the opportunity to talk about yourself and relate the issues and concerns you have had with your own hair. Be playful, make fun of yourself, and engage her to give you advice about what's hip. If the pink hair is a call for attention, the hair dialogue may be a nonthreatening way to get her to open up and discuss her feelings.

Hair Care Basics

In my research, I interviewed several hair stylists, did a ton of research, and learned many interesting facts about different hair textures, products, and styling. Though I've been in the beauty and fashion industry for many years and should have known better, I believed much of what I saw on TV. For instance, we see shampoo commercials with girls lathering up their hair and think that the foam is an indication that the product is working well. In actuality, lots of lather means the shampoo contains harsh detergents, which may strip hair of moisture. Furthermore, all those products that promise to add shine to the hair do not work if hair is not styled or blown dry properly. To save you time and money while also making sure you get the most out of the products you purchase, I have compiled a list of hair care facts to help you understand what is real and what is marketing. So let's jump right into it with hair washing.

SHAMPOO

Moms often ask me how often their daughters should shampoo.

The answer is that it really depends on the hair type and texture. Many hairdressers recommend that girls with thick curly hair or ethnic hair not shampoo daily. You may think hair is not getting clean if it's just rinsed with water, but warm water gets rid of some of the dirt and oil. Over-shampooing could dry out the hair and make it coarse and brittle. However, for other types of hair (especially limp or fine hair), daily washing is preferable so the oil does not weigh down hair and make it flat. You should experiment with your daughter's hair and decide what is best for her.

It is really important to find the right shampoo for your daughter. This may take some trial and error. Remember, do not make the mistake of judging the quality of a shampoo by the lather. When the shampoo produces lots of lather, it is due to the surfactants in the shampoo, the ingredients that cleanse the oil and dirt from hair. Harsher surfactants lather well but strip the hair.

Mild surfactants, such as betaines, will not produce a lot of lather, but they will help maintain a healthy balance of oil in your daughter's hair. If your daughter has finer hair, look for a product that adds volume. If her hair has more body, try a product designed to decrease frizz. If she swims a lot, use a clarifying shampoo formulated to wash out chlorine. I love the L'Oréal Kids line of shampoos. They are well priced, smell great, and are gentle on the eyes. Plus, you can buy a few different scents so your girl can alternate each time she washes her hair. L'Oréal Kids also makes Swim & Sport shampoo, which removes chlorine and minerals.

Generally, you should *avoid* two-in-one products that claim to shampoo and condition. They are never as effective as using separate products for cleaning and conditioning. Shampoo washes out the conditioner while conditioner weakens the shampoo.

CONDITIONING HAIR

Using conditioner can increase shine because it smoothes the hair cuticle. The deeper the conditioner, the smoother it will make the hair because it will add weight so hair lays down flat. If you just use shampoo, there will be more flyaway pieces of hair. Typically, the only difference among conditioners, finishing rinses, leave-in conditioners, and deep conditioners is the concentration of the active ingredients. However, the same ingredients usually exist in each.

Interestingly enough, the way a conditioner is used will determine the result. If a detangler or regular conditioner is left on the hair for a few minutes, it will smooth the hair cuticle. Deep conditioners get the best results if they are left on for fifteen to thirty minutes and are used with applied heat. Heat helps open the hair shaft to allow the conditioner to work on the hair. A rinse with cool water closes the hair shaft and boosts shine. Keep in mind that no product—even a deep conditioner—can fix split ends. The only way to get rid of split ends is to trim them.

Hair Growth and Health

Did you know that it is normal to lose between 50 and 150 hairs each day? Did you also know that hair grows faster during the summer due to the heat? On average, hair grows about six inches per year.

Need to Know

Conditioner—A product used after shampooing to detangle hair, improve texture and manageability, and decrease static. Conditioners are categorized as deep/heavy or finishing/light (definitions of each type follow in this alphabetized list).

Deep conditioner—A conditioner generally used with applied heat that penetrates the hair shaft to smooth damaged hair. They come in the form of creams, protein packs, hair masks, and hot oil treatments.

Detangling spray—A light spray applied to hair when wet to make it easier to comb.

Finishing rinse—A light formula of conditioner that coats the hair cuticle but does not penetrate the hair shaft. It is used to detangle hair without weighing the hair down.

Gel—A product that gives hair support and makes it easier to mold into the style you want. After it dries, however, it often leaves hair hard and crunchy if it is not distributed evenly throughout the hair or an improper amount is used.

Hair spray—A liquid sprayed on dry hair that keeps ends and style in place and smooths flyaway hair. A polymer-based hair spray will give hair a shine.

Leave-in conditioner—A conditioning product that is not rinsed out of the hair.

Mousse—A foamy product that works much like a gel. A touch of mousse added to wet hair helps hold the hairstyle you want. Mousse is also used to create flexible volume and body.

Pomade—A silicone-based product that has a waxier texture than gel does and contains no alcohol. It is sometimes referred to as hair wax. It offers less support than hair spray or other products, but it leaves hair supple and gives it a shiny, groomed look.

Shampoo—A soap-based product that washes out dirt, oil, and styling products.

Two-in-one shampoo and conditioner—One product that is supposed to act as both a shampoo and a conditioner.

Volumizing sprays—Sprays that plump up limp hair, curls, and waves. They straighten ethnic hair and tame frizzies. Use a volumizing spray on wet hair before styling, and apply it to the roots when hair is dry.

John Barrett Product Tips

Everything in moderation! Experiment with small amounts of product until you know how it will work in your daughter's hair.

Touchability is key. If another person touches your daughter's hair and says "Eew, gross!" she has used too much product. If hair is brittle and crunchy, excessively greasy, or stains clothes, either she has used too much and/or it's not a good product for her hair.

Shine, which we normally associate with healthy hair, comes from the reflection of light off a smooth surface. The smoother the surface, the greater the shine. Think of how shiny a smooth lake is as opposed to the wavy surface of the ocean. Frizzy hairs and damaged strands of hair are like the waves of the ocean. They prevent light from reflecting off the hair surface, inhibiting shine. Shampoos and conditioners may help to smooth hair and give you some shine, but for truly shiny hair it is necessary to use styling tools and products that will make hair appear smoother and shinier.

Styling Tools You May Need

Have you ever seen what happens when you brush curly hair? It loses its curl, there is no shine, and it becomes big and fluffy. Not pretty. Not all hair should be brushed. The most important factor in making any hair beautiful is having the right tools on hand. The styling tools discussed here will give you an idea of what is available, but the most important thing to remember is to buy the tools that are right for your daughter's hair.

COMBS

There are many types of combs, each with a different purpose. With all the combs available on the market, I think it is best to get one plastic wide-toothed comb and one metal teasing comb. Only use a comb on wet hair. Expert John Barrett says a brush will break and damage wet hair. Although wood combs look beautiful, they are not great for use on wet hair unless they are sealed to ward off moisture.

A Wide-Toothed Comb

I think everyone should have a wide-toothed comb. With its rounded edges, a wide-toothed comb can be used daily on all hair types. It tames hair without catching on every knot or split end. This type of comb is inexpensive and readily available in drugstores and supermarkets.

After shampooing, have your daughter put conditioner on her hair and leave it in for a few minutes. Give her a plastic wide-toothed comb to work the conditioner through the ends and smooth away the tangles. After she rinses out the conditioner she should towel dry her hair and then comb her hair to ensure all the knots are out.

Combs with a Long Tip for Parts and Teasing

There are combs that come with a long metal or plastic tip at the end. Because they have a pointed edge, they are great for teasing hair and making parts for ponytails and braids. Simply take the metal end and draw a line down from her crown to the nape of her neck to create a perfect part.

BRUSHES

A brush should have no "return," which means the needles should not go back down into the brush and come up through a different hole. (Brushes with a return are especially rough on hair because the short needle, which sticks up from the second hole, is sharp and will cut and snag hair.) Always look for a brush with individual needles and rounded tips.

Natural Fiber Brushes

Natural fiber brushes are made of boar bristles, which are the gentlest on hair and last forever. I recommend natural brushes for your daughter if she has a sensitive scalp or hair that is prone to knotting. Using a natural brush will not pull her hair and hurt her scalp like a synthetic brush will. Mason Pearson makes a wonderful child-sensitive boar bristle brush. Though it is a bit costly (about $80), you will have it forever, and it will not hurt your daughter's head. It's the only brush my daughter will let me use on her hair.

Synthetic Brushes

Brushes made of synthetic materials (plastic) are less gentle on the hair, but they also minimize static.

Paddle Brushes

A paddle brush is a flat, wide brush; it is excellent for thick hair that is difficult to comb through. It is used to create smooth styles without frizz. My favorite paddle brush is the Aveda Wooden Paddle Brush (about $18). It brushes through hair easily while gently massaging the scalp.

Round Brushes

For blow-drying hair, round brushes are best. They come in various sizes—smaller for tighter curls, larger for looser curls.

Some round brushes come with a clip to hold hair in place as you blow-dry each section. Most round brushes are synthetic and can catch hair or be difficult to pull out as you blow-dry. Hard plastic bristles can be quite harsh; try a brush with softer bristles.

HAIR DRYER AND DIFFUSER

Hair dryers do not generally last more than four years. I recommend a hair dryer with hot and cool settings, a hook to hang it on, and an attach-on nozzle to keep your daughter from burning her hair. I recommend a dryer with 1,600–2,000 watts. (Note: Try to find one in a pretty color that matches the bathroom.) For curly hair, attach a diffuser with "fingers" to the dryer. The diffuser will keep hair from frizzing and lift and separate the curls.

CURLERS/CURLING IRON

Hot rollers should have foam around them to protect hair from burning. To add natural body and waves, Velcro rollers are the way to go. For individual ringlets and ethnic hair, a curling iron is preferable.

FLAT IRON

A flat iron is used to straighten all types of hair. It can be used on straight and wavy hair to make it even straighter. It is also a great tool for ethnic hair because it allows you to smooth the hair without harsh chemical relaxers. Use cooler settings for straighter and wavier hair types and hotter settings for thicker or curlier hair. Look for a flat iron in which the part that gets hot is made of ceramic not aluminum because ceramic is less damaging to the hair.

ACCESSORIES

Covered elastic bands are great for ponytails, braids, and chignons. Rubber bands destroy, tear, tangle, and split hair. However, rubber bands may be used on ethnic hair when adding beads to braids. They should be cut out with a scissor so as not to break the hair.

Barrettes and bobby pins hold back bangs or layers. Barrettes can be visible, but bobby pins should be hidden. For pinning curls, small bobby pins are best. For chignons and French twists, use larger ones; they will hold the hair better.

Combs and headbands hold hair that is growing out or tends to be unruly. A pretty comb or a headband keeps hair off the face.

Caring for and Styling All Types of Hair

If you think every female should wash her hair daily, brush it one hundred times each night, and trim it every six weeks, you are wrong. One size does not fit all when it comes to a hair care regimen. There are many types of hair: straight, wavy, curly, and variations of all three. Each hair type requires something different. For instance, you can brush straight hair and come out with a beautiful, neat head of hair. Use that same brush on curly hair and you will have a big fluffy mess with no curl or shine. I know it's hard for you as a mom to imagine not brushing your daughter's hair, but sometimes, brushing is exactly what you should not do.

The next section details the basics for washing, caring, and styling the most common hair types. I have outlined some basic guidelines for girls of all ethnic backgrounds. Hair care expert Ellin LaVar, who has a fabulous salon in New York, encourages moms not to treat hair according to skin color but according to texture. It is always best to find a salon that specializes in your daughter's hair texture. Find a stylist who can help you manage her hair and instruct you on the best products to use. The Internet is a great resource to consult in finding the best salons in your area.

CURLY, FRIZZY HAIR

Curly, frizzy hair is the most difficult hair to care for and style. As a result, most girls with this type of hair are always trying to straighten it. However, your daughter can wear her curly hair natural and look beautiful just by making a few changes to her daily

To Blow-dry, Curl, and Flat Iron All Hair Types

To Blow-Dry Hair

1. Towel dry wet hair and comb through the tangles. If hair has lots of tangles, spray L'Oréal Kids Tangle Tamer all over hair before combing. For coarse hair, Ellin LaVar recommends combing out the tangles at the bottom of the hair before the ones closer to the crown.

2. Separate a section of hair. Grab it by the bottom. Insert the brush (use either a medium size round brush or a brush attachment on your dryer) at the top of the hair near the scalp and slide it down to the end of the hair section as you are blow-drying the hair. For a straighter look, use a large round brush.

3. Do this section by section until you have finished.

4. Spray a light-mist hair spray all over. Make sure to hold the spray bottle or can ten inches from the hair to coat it evenly and avoid crunchy spots. Comb through once with a wide-toothed comb.

Go to www.conair.com for a great instructional video.

To Curl Hair

For limp, fine hair, be sure hair is clean and not weighed down with gels and mousses. When using hot rollers, leave them in for three minutes for a looser curl and for ten to fifteen minutes for a tighter, longer-lasting curl.

1. Pull a section (finger width) of dry, clean hair out at a right angle from the scalp. For example, if you are curling a piece on top, pull the hair straight up. If you are curling a piece on the side, pull hair straight out parallel to the floor.

2. Place any type of roller at the tips of the hair and roll it back halfway to the scalp. You can experiment with hot rollers to see if you get the desired result.

3. Secure roller with a clip.

4. Leave rollers in for ten to twenty minutes.

5. Unroll the curlers.

Go to www.Spindaily.com to watch a great video on how to use hot rollers.

To Flat Iron Hair

To flat iron ethnic hair or hair that tends to be coarse, kinky, curly, or frizzy, I like to apply Ellin LaVar PenetratingBalm because it makes hair soft, not greasy. You can apply it to clean hair before you iron it. Hair will come out soft and bouncy When flat ironing, she recommends you do not do more than one finger width of hair per section. The smaller the section, the smoother the hair. For hair that is mostly straight, with just a little bit of wave, you can flat iron without product in the hair.

1. Pull a section of hair out straight. For example, if you are flat ironing a section on top, pull the hair straight up. If you are flat ironing a piece on the side, pull hair straight out parallel to the floor.

2. Take a flat iron and pull down the section of hair from the root to the tip.

3. Repeat with each section of hair.

Go to www.conair.com to see instructional videos on how to use a flat iron.

hair care routine. John Barrett says the key is to not touch the hair after it is styled, which is often difficult for younger girls. Nevertheless, try to get your daughter to keep her hands out of her hair once the two of you have styled it.

Washing

- Two to three times per week shampoo and rinse. After showering, apply a mixture of leave-in conditioner and pomade to curls.
- Two to three times per week rinse hair with water only. Apply a mixture of leave-in conditioner and pomade to curls while hair is wet.
- Once a week leave a deep conditioner in hair for twenty minutes under heat, then rinse.

Trimming

With curly hair, I recommend your daughter keep it long. Length weighs down the curls so hair is heavier and less frizzy. Do not trim curly hair every six weeks. Because curly hair scrunches up like a corkscrew, a one-inch trim can look like a three-inch haircut. Only trim split ends when it is absolutely necessary, which may only be two to four times per year.

Styling

To tame curls:

1. Mix a dime-size amount of pomade with leave-in conditioner. (The hold from the pomade plus the weight of the conditioner will tame curls.)

2. Smooth the mixture through the hair, section by section, from the roots to the ends of the hair.
3. Using a comb or fingers, put each curl into place.
4. Do not touch it! Frizz occurs when hair is handled during the drying process. If you leave it alone, the curl pattern will stay in tact.

To make hair straighter but still keep some body, follow the instructions for blow-drying hair and then follow it up with a flat iron.

Styling Curls for Special Events

The preteen years are right about the time that girls start going to coed parties. There may also be special family- or community-oriented events she must attend. It is always nice to do something a little special for your daughter, especially if the occasion is a birthday, a religious event, or a party.

1. Flip wet hair upside down, and smooth the pomade-conditioner mixture through it.
2. Blow-dry hair with a diffuser attached, scrunching sections of hair as you work through section by section.
3. Flip hair back. Curls should be wild and glamorous.

Semipermanent Straightening for Curly Hair and Ethnic Hair

I believe it is best to teach your daughter to embrace the hair she was born with and learn how to style it properly. But if her hair is taking over her life and just never looks the way she likes it, many salons offer Japanese straightening, thermal reconditioning, straight perms, and Brazilian keratin treatments. John Barrett recommends not using a chemical straightener on your preteen's hair because the treatment is too harsh and will damage the hair texture. Ellin LaVar says that chemically straightening a young girl's hair, especially trying it at home, can damage the hair cuticle. I am not advocating chemical straightening, although I feel you should know about it in case it is something you and your daughter are seriously considering. Brazilian keratin treatments do a nice job smoothing the cuticle and making hair soft and more manageable, however, some contain formaldehyde. It washes out over time and lasts about three months.

Japanese Yuko straightening is a chemical process that contains formaldehyde. It makes hair stick-straight and lasts for about six months. After this process, your daughter will be able to wash her hair and go without much fuss. However, the process is costly and, since hair can be easily burned and destroyed, you must go to a reputable salon with lots of experience using these products. For ethnic hair straightening, the chemicals can also be too harsh and destroy the hair. If you choose to do it, follow up with regular weekly deep conditioning treatments in a salon. If you are interested, go online and do lots of research to find a good salon within your budget.

ETHNIC HAIR

Ethnic hair can range from curly, thick, or tightly woven curls to straight and fine. If your daughter's hair texture is different from your own, it might be challenging to know exactly which hair products and styles will work best in her hair. According to Nicolie McNeil of Ebony Styles International Salon, it is important to find a stylist who will help you keep your daughter's hair healthy. Proper conditioning and using products with natural oils and butters is the best way to keep ethnic hair hydrated and healthy. Ellin LaVar recommends limiting shampooing to once per week to maintain the oil in the hair.

Washing

- Once per week, shampoo and rinse. Use deep conditioner formulated for ethnic hair every time hair is washed if hair is tightly coiled. Regular conditioner is fine for finer hair.
- Once per week apply a hair mask or deep conditioner with natural butters. Leave in for ten minutes under a shower cap. Rinse.

Trimming

Ethnic hair only needs to be trimmed when you see split ends or when chemical straightening has damaged hair. Trim hair as needed.

Styling

Be careful not to complain that your tween's hair is too difficult or unmanageable. It is important that she embrace her natural beauty. Try out some of these simple styles and talk to your daughter while you style her hair. Be sure to tell her how much fun it is to play with and style her hair.

Hairstyles

Here are two types of hairstyles for your daughter to try out:

Two-Strand Twists

1. Use a detangler to comb through clean wet hair.
2. Make small parts through her hair.
3. Take two strands of hair and twist from root to end.
4. Untie twists in a few days for a different look and hold back hair with a headband.

Braids

When braiding a child's hair, Nicolie McNeil recommends you use only the child's natural hair. Adding extra hair/extensions to the braid will make the braid too tight and can hurt the child's head. If extra hair is ever added to a hairstyle, it must be human hair not synthetic. If you decide to use beads at the end of the braid, Nicolie McNeil says too many beads can weigh down hair and hurt the hair follicle.

1. Wash hair and use a detangler to comb through clean wet hair.
2. Blow-dry hair. You can moisturize the scalp but do not grease the hair.
3. Make small parts through her hair.
4. Braid small or large braids depending on your preference.
5. If you choose to add beads at the end of the braid, be sure the end of the braid is small enough to fit through the bead. Once hair is braided, add as many beads as desired. When you get to the last bead, put the end of the hair over the bead and put a small rubber band on it.

Straightening

As I stated earlier, the consensus among hairdressers I interviewed is to avoid chemically processing a child's hair—especially
at home. At home, it is so easy to overprocess hair, which makes
it brittle and unhealthy. A better alternative is to use a flat iron.
Purchase a flat iron made from toumaline ceramic. It straightens
hair quickly, imparts moisture, and takes away excess heat. This
all-natural alternative to chemical straightening keeps hair healthy
and does not activate possible allergic reactions in the scalp.

If you decide to chemically straighten hair, it should only be
done in a salon and followed up by deep conditioning treatments
in a salon where they use professional products and applied heat.

Weaving and Extensions

Weaving and extensions are costly and time-consuming, but many
young girls love them. If your daughter is begging to try them,
buy her inexpensive clip-on extensions that she can play with at
home. If you choose to give her a weave or extensions, take her to
a reputable salon and ask the cost of maintenance and whether it
will hurt your daughter's head. Then make an informed decision
with your daughter.

STRAIGHT HAIR AND WAVY HAIR

If your daughter has straight or wavy hair, washing and styling it is
pretty straightforward. However, straight hair can vary from being
stick-straight to wavy if it is not blown-dry. Oftentimes, spaghetti-
straight hair, which always looks shiny, has little body. Then there
is straight hair that tends to be a bit messy looking if air-dried.

There is also hair that is wavy when air-dried but straightens easily when blow-dried. Whichever type she has, these basic tips will help you style it so she feels her best.

Washing Straight Hair That Waves if It's Not Blown-dry
This type of hair is easy to care for because it can be washed as often as you like. If her hair tends to get greasy and flat, wash more frequently.

- Three to seven times per week shampoo and rinse. Use a conditioner or finishing rinse and leave in hair for three to five minutes. Rinse.
- Once per week or every other week use a deep conditioner and leave it in hair for twenty minutes under a warm towel. Rinse.

Washing Limp, Straight Hair
Limp hair needs to be washed more often to keep the natural oils from weighing it down. If hair gets too dry from daily washing, you may need to switch to a more gentle shampoo. Spray wet hair with a volumizer for maximum body. Do not use shampoos with built-in conditioners. Do not use leave-in conditioners. They will make hair heavy and even more limp. If the hair needs some conditioning, use a finishing rinse, but only on the ends.

- Five to seven times per week shampoo and rinse.
- Use a finishing rinse only on the ends of the hair. Rinse it out.

Trimming

Straight hair may be trimmed every four to six weeks or when you notice split ends. Generally, straight hair worn in a blunt, even cut benefits from more frequent trimming to keep the shape of the hairstyle.

Wavy hair may be trimmed less often because a one-inch trim can look like two inches when hair is dry. Trim wavy hair when it needs to be shaped or when you see split ends.

Styling with Rollers

For instant body, try hot rollers. For tighter waves, use smaller sections of hair and curlers smaller in circumference. For looser waves, use larger curlers and larger sections of hair.

1. Make sure hair is completely dry. Take a section of hair and pull it out at a ninety-degree angle from the scalp. For example, if you are curling a piece on top, pull the hair straight up. If you are curling a piece on the side, pull hair straight out parallel to the floor.
2. Put a hot roller on the underside of the ends.
3. Carefully roll it back until it is in a tight curl on the scalp and secure it with curl holder.

Go to www.spindaily.com for a great instructional video.

Styling with a Curling Iron

For tighter curls or bottle curls, use a curling iron. Curling irons take longer, but they give you more control over each strand of hair.

1. Grasp the end of the hair in between the curling iron and the movable clip and curl hair around the iron in the same direction. If you switch direction, you will fold the hair over the clip, creating a crease in the hair.
2. Hold for twenty seconds or more (depending on how well hair holds the curl) and release.

For a comprehensive instructional video, see www.conairyoucurl.com.

Styling with Pin Curls

To create looser, more natural-looking curls, use pin curls. Ehow. com has an easy-to-follow instructional video you can watch to really get an understanding of how easy it is to do a pin curl.

1. Take a small section (about thirty hairs) of damp hair.
2. With the right hand, bend the end of the hair around the left index finger and roll the hair around your finger until you reach the top of the head.
3. Secure the curl with a bobby pin going through the hole of the curl.
4. Do the whole head and let your daughter sleep on it.

COLOR-TREATED HAIR

Hopefully, your daughter's hair is healthy. Many young girls experiment with color and end up destroying their hair. If your daughter comes home from a sleepover with hair that's three shades lighter and fried on the ends, or if she convinced you to let her get a perm, here is how to treat it.

Hair Washing

- The number of times the hair should be washed depends on the hair type. Wash hair with a color-safe shampoo. Use a color-safe conditioner and leave it in for three to five minutes. Rinse.
- Once a week use a deep conditioning treatment for processed hair and leave it in for ten to twenty minutes under a warm towel. Rinse.

Hair Trimming

Color-treated hair tends to get damaged more quickly due to the chemicals in hair color. Trim hair every four to six weeks to keep it healthy and remove split ends.

Protecting the Color

- Use styling products (not shampoos) with UV protection.
- At the beach, have her use a leave-in conditioner or pomade to lock the moisture in hair.
- Before she dives into a pool, saturate her hair with freshwater or club soda. (This is great under a swim cap when she is doing laps.) The hair is like a hole. If you fill it up with water or club soda, the chlorine can't get in to the cuticle and damage her hair.
- Give her frequent hair treatments and massage her scalp before bed.
- Avoid perming and coloring during her period. Professionals say it doesn't matter, but from personal experience with my test group and myself, hair just does not seem to color or perm as well—or maybe it's our skewed perception. Whatever it is, I don't recommend it.

Deep Conditioning

Salons charge a lot of money to deep condition hair because they use professional products and they have big hair dryers to apply heat. If this is beyond your budget, ask your daughter's stylist how to deep condition her hair at home. Ellin LaVar recommends working a deep conditioner through the hair and covering it with a shower cap. Then wrap aluminum foil around the cap to lock in the heat and keep it confined.

Go to the drugstore or salon and buy a deep conditioning treatment or mask. (For ethnic hair, buy the deep conditioning treatment your hair care professional recommends.) You can spend as little or as much as you want depending on your budget. Deep conditioners can be found in individual packets, or you can buy a whole bottle. If all else fails, use your normal conditioner and follow these directions:

1. Shampoo hair and towel dry.
2. Work the conditioner into hair.
3. Cover hair with a shower cap and then aluminum foil or a wet towel. (You can always heat the towel with a hair dryer while it is on your girl's head, or stick the towel in the microwave to heat it.) The heat opens the hair cuticles to allow the conditioner to penetrate the hair shaft.
4. If it is warm out, she can sit in the sun for twenty minutes.
5. After twenty minutes, she can wash out the conditioner.

HAIR WITH DANDRUFF

Many girls get dandruff in the winter. That isn't surprising because oftentimes dandruff is a result of stress or a change in seasons. Her scalp may be dry and school could be stressful enough to make those ugly flakes appear in the scalp. Dandruff is easily treated if she follows this regimen.

Hair Washing

- Three to five times per week have her use a dandruff shampoo every other time she washes her hair. Buy three different dandruff shampoos and alternate them each time she washes her hair.
- Use a moisturizing conditioner and leave it in for three to five minutes. Rinse.

She should not use a dandruff shampoo for more than two weeks. Even during these two weeks, alternate between the dandruff shampoo and a regular shampoo because dandruff shampoos can be harsh and strip the hair. Dandruff shampoo should contain zinc ammonium, the ingredient that cures dandruff. Avoid shampoos that smell too medicinal; these products are often overly harsh. If dandruff shampoos aren't working, Nioxin offers a line of shampoos that is designed to treat more severe skin and hair conditions and is well formulated to be gentle on the hair. If dandruff is a habitual problem, you may want to seek the help of a trichologist or dermatologist who can give your daughter a prescription shampoo.

LONG HAIR

There is nothing more fun than styling your daughter's hair. Here are some fun ideas to make her feel you are interested in her appearance. She will love having you do her hair and you will find it is a great way to get her to talk to you.

Hair Washing

Follow the instructions for your daughter's hair type. In general, if her hair is more oily, wash five to seven days per week followed by a light conditioner. For dryer hair, three to five times a week with a good conditioner should do the trick.

Hair Trimming

Follow the instructions for your daughter's hair type. But keep this in mind: long hair is only pretty when it is healthy. Long split ends are dead hair with no body or shine. It is better to cut a few inches and have healthy hair than to have long straggly dead hair.

Styling Hair

If your daughter has long hair that is very straight or soft, it may be difficult to style. Try teasing sections of hair before styling, styling it wet, or styling it a day or so after washing.

To tease

1. Lift a section of hair straight up from her head.
2. Holding hair ends, backcomb the hair from the end to the root. The section should look knotty and out of control. Spray volumizer or hair spray on the section.
3. Repeat step 2 with sections around the first teased section.

4. Lightly comb teased sections into desired style or proceed to create a more elaborate style like a French twist or chignon (described below). For more height, lift the hair sections higher with the pick end of the teasing comb.

See ehow.com for an easy to follow instructional video.

The Perfect Ponytail

John Barrett suggests making a ponytail and leaving a section of hair out at the bottom. Once the hair is secure, wrap that section around the ponytail and tuck the end into the elastic band. You could also leave the two front sections out, secure the ponytail with the elastic band, and then wrap one section around the ponytail, secure with bobby pin, and then do the same with the other section. It is such a great look!

French twist

1. Pull the long hair into a ponytail with your fingers. Make sure it is between the crown and the nape to get all the hair in.
2. Twist the ponytail all the way to the ends.
3. Pull the twist up the side opposite to the direction of the twist. (If you twisted clockwise, pull the twist up the left side.)
4. Tuck the twist under the opposite side of hair. Be sure to tuck

in any loose ends up top by simply pulling the ends around counterclockwise and then tucking them into the twist.

5. If you are using bobby pins, opt for larger ones and place them horizontally at the center underneath the twist so they are out of sight. Or use a pretty jaw clip scooping the twist between the two jaws to hold the twist in place.

6. Spray the twist for a better hold. Pull down some wisps to frame the face.

Chignon

1. Make a high ponytail with your daughter's hair by holding it with your right hand.

2. Wrap the ponytail around itself, and then pull the end up through the hole in the middle of the coil as if you were making a knot.

3. If hair does not stay by itself, use some bobby pins.

Or . . .

1. Make two low ponytails.

2. Twist the ponytails together. Wrap the twist around itself into a bun.

3. Experiment with bobby pins to keep the bun in place.

French braid

1. Take three sections of hair from the top of your preteen's head and braid them together twice.

2. When you come to braid it a third time, add some of the hair on the right side to the right piece of the braid.

3. Braid that piece in as you would normally.

4. Now before braiding in the left piece, take some hair from the left side and add it to the left piece.
5. Braid normally.
6. Continue this until there is no hair left to grab.
7. Finish the braid and secure with an elastic band.

SHORT HAIR

Short hair can look very chic on a young girl. It might seem like it's not as much fun to play with, but there are several things you can do with short hair.

Hair Washing

You can wash short hair as often as necessary. If hair is very straight, daily washing is best. For a messier look, she can wash it less often.

Accessorize

A fun mother-daughter activity, no matter how long or short your daughter's hair or what her hair type, could be a simple shopping trip to the mall. Almost every mall has a Claire's boutique, and what girl doesn't love Claire's? Get some great headbands, barrettes, and little butterfly clips. Then go home and play. Even if the style is not something she would necessarily go out in, your focus is on her and making her feel special. Plus, it's so much fun!

Hair Trimming

Short hairstyles need to be trimmed every four to six weeks to maintain the style and shape of the cut.

Hair Styling

Slick it back

1. Put a dime-size amount of gel in your palm, rub both palms together, and work gel through damp hair.
2. Comb into place.

Tousle it

1. Put a dime-size amount of gel in your palm, rub both palms together, and work gel through damp hair.
2. Mess up her hair with both hands.

Curl it

A curling iron will give you control over how much curl you want. It can also add body to short hair and give your little beauty a completely different look.

Finding a Stylist and Colorist

The hardest part of getting a great haircut or great color (addressed in more detail in the next section) is finding the right person to do it. Don't you just love those high-tech salons that serve you espresso and chocolates, which you choke on when you see the three-digit bill and poodle-haircut some sadistic stylist gave your daughter?

John Barrett suggests you find the best place for yourself and a stylist you trust. Do not make your daughter be the guinea pig by trying a hairdresser you do not know. If your budget allows, take your daughter to the salon you use. Then let your daughter explain her ideas of fabulous to the hairdresser. The stylist could be quite helpful in negotiating a style that is pleasing to both of you.

If your salon is out of budget for your daughter, try a walk-in salon at the mall. Before going to a stylist, look at the client the stylist just finished to get an idea of his/her work. Or just get a shampoo and blow-dry to see if your daughter is comfortable with the stylist. No matter what your budget, the rules on the following page apply across the board.

CONSULTATIONS

The best salons give prospective clients free consultations. Think of it as an interview: you're the boss with no obligation to hire anyone. Try this at a few different places and see if there is a consensus.

Consult with a stylist specializing in what you want. If it's a cut, don't see a do-it-all who cuts, colors, and perms.

Have your daughter bring in pictures of what she likes and doesn't like. Pictures should resemble her hair type. The pictures should be of a style she could realistically achieve not just a model or actress she tries to emulate. If her expectations are within the realm of reality, she will be happier with the outcome.

Find out the price, including tax and tip. Many places give student discounts; don't be shy about asking for one.

Make sure the stylist can communicate with you. If you feel uncomfortable, you should promptly leave. Do not be intimidated or feel you need to trust this person just because you had a consultation.

Rules for Finding the Right Stylist for Your Daughter

1. John Barrett says if you see someone with a great haircut/ hairdo or color, stop her on the street and ask who does her hair.

2. Tweet or call beauty and lifestyle editors of your local papers. Go to a salon they recommend, get an impression, and find a stylist who agrees with you and your daughter and will give you both what you want.

3. Don't let an androgynous-looking stylist with a purple Mohawk and black lipstick cut your sweet daughter's blonde bob. Your visions of beauty are probably quite different. Also, make sure that your daughter is comfortable with the stylist you choose.

4. Avoid your sister's friend's uncle's niece who just graduated from beauty school. Let her practice on somebody else.

5. Get your daughter a free consultation at the salon. (You should never pay for a consultation.) Look at the clients as they leave the salon. If they look like your grandmother, you may be at the wrong place.

6. For ethnic hair, Nicolie McNeil advises against a stylist who immediately wants to relax your child's hair. Instead, speak to a stylist who is knowledgeable about hair care and whose goal is to keep your daughter's hair healthy.

7. Choose a stylist with hair similar to your daughter's hair. If she has curly hair, try to find someone with the same type of hair. That stylist will probably be more understanding than someone with spaghetti-straight locks.

THE HAIRCUT RULES

Here are some foolproof rules to get the best haircut for your daughter:

1. If your daughter wears makeup, have her wear it the way she normally does when leaving the house.
2. Don't go to the salon with her dressed like a rocker if she normally likes to look preppy. The hairdresser will misinterpret her style and give her a cut she is uncomfortable with.
3. Avoid the loving-your-cut-until-you-wash-it syndrome. If she spends only five minutes a day on her hair, say so! Ask for a low-maintenance cut.
4. Discuss how often you will have to get her hair cut. If you want to bring her in once every two months, do not get a short stylish haircut, which will need to be reshaped in four weeks.
5. Tell her to sit with good posture and uncrossed legs. Crossed legs throw one shoulder lower than the other, which may result in an uneven cut.
6. Insist that your daughter sit still! Once a hairdresser cut my hair three inches shorter than I had wanted, and I complained. Her reply? "You turned your head so many times, I made a mistake and had to even it out."
7. If you are going to have a say in the style, avoid using technical terms like "shoulder length" or "the shag." John Barrett says shoulder length means something different to everyone. Describe what you want by placing a comb at the point where you want the hair to fall.

8. This is your daughter's hair. Do not let her be scared or intimidated by the hairdresser. If you or your daughter does not like something, tell the stylist. After all, you will be drying the tears when you get home.

9. Tell her to keep her hands out of her hair while it's being cut. The stylist has a very sharp instrument and can't use it properly if your tween is constantly playing with her hair.

10. "Just do whatever you want" is the worst thing to tell a hairdresser. Take some responsibility for the haircut and give the stylist an idea of what you and your daughter want.

HAIR COLOR

Although you may not want to color your daughter's beautiful hair, she might feel otherwise. I encourage you to do your best to get her to keep her hair natural as long as possible. All the chemicals in hair dyes are damaging to the hair and they penetrate the scalp. However, she is growing up, and if you have a tween who is verging on becoming a teen, she might have a different idea of what color she wants her hair to be.

The most important thing to remember about color is that it goes through stages. Changing hair color is like looking at a chart that goes from white to black. If you have brown hair and want to go blonde, the color will first change from brown to red. Next it will be golden red, and then finally blonde. However, many people panic when they're applying hair color at home, and they rinse it off too soon. That is why you see girls with crazy colors. If your daughter really wants to change her hair color, I suggest you go to a salon to get the color she wants. Discuss maintenance and budget with the colorist before you color.

If a salon is out of your budget, at-home hair color kits are a great way to color hair four shades lighter or darker than your teen's actual color. These kits are inexpensive and easy to use. You also have the option to start with semipermanent dyes or henna before taking the big step to permanent color. However, I do not suggest them for more extreme changes. If budget is a concern, do not do anything drastic. While that little box of hair color may not cost much, fixing it in the salon can cost hundreds of dollars.

John Barrett encourages moms to compromise and negotiate. Instead of agreeing to make your brunette daughter platinum, take her with you when you get your hair done. Ask the colorist to highlight a couple of strands of your daughter's hair so she feels she has done something. My eight-year-old was desperate to have blonde hair like me. She has the most beautiful brown hair you have ever seen. So, finally, I let my colorist do a small piece of blonde in her hair. While I could barely see it, my daughter was thrilled and felt really grown up.

HAIR COLORING GUIDE

Go to www.garnierusa.com for a step-by-step instructional video to apply hair color.

Permanent color

A permanent color normally uses 20-volume peroxide to go lighter and 10-volume peroxide to go darker. The products sold in stores are 10–15 volume, which is why you have to leave them in an extra five minutes. Permanent color will last until the new hair grows in.

The peroxide opens the hair shaft, allows the color to enter, and locks in the color. Although the color result is permanent, root

Rules for Doing Basic Color at Home

1. Don't look at the picture on the box. (Her hair will never match the color of the woman's hair on the box.)

2. You can't lighten hair with a tint; you must use bleach. It's like painting; you have to add white to make it lighter. That being said, *never* put bleach on your child's hair at home. You can burn her scalp, hair can break off, and the color could be disastrous.

3. Always do a test section (about twenty individual strands in a clump) and record how long it takes to get hair to the desired color.

4. Before buying a product, call the toll-free hotline on the back of the box. A professional can help you choose the right color.

5. To go darker, use an ammonia-free, peroxide-free semipermanent color. They are easier to play with in terms of color. In case you do not like the color, it will be gone in six to eight washings.

6. For coloring especially long hair, buy two packages of color so you do not run out in the middle.

7. You should apply the color for your daughter with the applicator bottle so you get an even, complete application.

8. Test the product on her inner arm twenty-four hours before dyeing her hair to assure that she is not allergic to the chemicals.

9. Apply Vaseline around hairline and ears to keep color from staining the skin.

10. Choose either to color or to perm the hair, not both. Doing both processes will destroy the hair.

11. Follow timing instructions on the box and add an extra five minutes. This will not hurt the hair. Do not do it for less time than is specified because you will not get the desired color.

touch-ups are required every four to six weeks depending on how fast the hair grows.

Semipermanent Color

A semipermanent color uses no ammonia and only low peroxide. This color should wash out after shampooing between six and eight times. However, there is a chance the color will not wash out due to the low levels of peroxide. If you do not want to take this chance, choose a product with no peroxide.

Henna

Henna is a safe, natural way to color your daughter's hair. The great thing about henna is that it does not have harsh chemicals and will wash out in six to eight weeks. It is really more like a semipermanent color than anything else. Because there are special ways to apply henna, you must consult the product you choose for directions.

Going Darker

To make your tween's hair up to four shades darker, you can use an at-home color kit. If it's her first time, start with a semipermanent color or henna. That way, if she hates the color or you distribute the color unevenly, she won't have to live with it for very long.

Going Blonde

If your daughter has dark hair and wants to be blonde, do not color her hair at home. I guarantee it will turn orange and she will hate it. Have a free consultation with a colorist at a salon and find out how much it will cost to color the hair and then maintain it. Typically, the single process (roots only) will have to be done once per month, and the highlights once every three to six months.

If she is already blonde and wants to lighten her hair and a salon is out of your price range, call the hotline number on the package of an at-home coloring product. Ask a color-consultant for help in choosing the color right for her hair.

Going Red

Red at home is risky because there are so many shades of red, and most of us are not expert enough to know how the color will react to our natural hair color. Even for professionals, red hair is the hardest color to achieve. If a salon is out of your budget, do not do red. If you just want to add a red glimmer, buy a shampoo that adds color until the next washing.

Highlighting

Highlighting is a process that adds lighter shades to any color. Highlights should catch the light and make hair appear shiny and bright. Your best bet for perfect highlighting is going to a salon. You need an experienced professional who will use different shades in different places.

Highlighting tends to run between $100 and $600 depending on how much you have done and what salon you go to. Touch-ups need to be done every three to six months.

You can choose from a few other options, however, if those prices are out of your comfort zone. You can try an at-home highlighting product. For best results, do a test strand and time how long it takes to reach the desired color. Then, do the rest of the hair, leaving color on for the same amount of time as you did for the test strand. If you go this route, just do six small clumps of hair, about twenty strands each. Imagine drawing a few rays of sunshine from the top of your daughter's head down through her hair. When doing the rest of her hair, don't get carried away and put in too many highlights just because you liked the first few. The result will be to have the highlighting look fake. The purpose of highlights is to give a look of naturally beautiful hair.

Lowlights

For light hair, you can add darker color for more contrast. These are called lowlights. They will darken hair the way highlights will lighten hair.

* * *

I hope you enjoyed trying some of the techniques in this chapter. When you spend time on your girl's hair, you are telling her she is important. Her hair is often a subject that either makes her feel happy or makes her feel insecure. Her frustration with her look will manifest itself in her self-esteem. I have a friend who always hated her curly hair because it was so unmanageable. When she finally found a stylist who taught her how to care for it and make the curls soft and supple in the summer and straight with a flat iron in the winter, her whole personality changed. She felt more confident in her look.

Hair color can also change a girl's image. If your older tween is a mousy dark blonde, a few highlights to brighten her up may bring the shy girl out of her shell. I am not suggesting platinum by any means. But don't be afraid to make a change if her current style or color is not working for her.

If she is unhappy with her look, simply cutting waist-length hair to the shoulders and donating the hair to children with cancer can change her look and do some good for another child. Growing out bangs or buying a new barrette can update her image. The best thing you can do is to take an interest in your daughter's hair and help her find the most flattering look for her, not you. Be flexible. Hair grows back. Nothing is forever except the bond the two of you form now.

Bonding Activities

- If it's summertime and you are going to the beach, John Barrett suggests you both go to the your local mall or pharmacy and buy a hair mask (also called hydrating or nourishment masks) specifically formulated for the hair type you and your daughter have. Before going down to the beach each day, work a little bit of mask through your hair, from the roots to the tips. Pull hair into a ponytail and let the heat of the sun activate the deep conditioning of the mask. After an hour or two or even when you get home, wash it out.
- In the wintertime, do the same thing with the hair mask, only this time use hot towels to wrap up your hair and relax and watch a movie or TV together while hair is deep conditioning. You can also listen to music together and talk about her and what is going on in her life.

- Take a trip to the salon together to get your hair done. After your day of beauty, take her to lunch and talk about the experience.
- If she is desperate for highlights, go to a salon or buy an at-home highlighting kit and paint in six highlights from root to tip. Highlights should be no more than four shades lighter than her actual hair color.
- Before bed, put her clean hair in several braids around her head. In the morning, undo the braids for a wavy look.
- On the weekend, take her to get some fun accessories for her hair.
- Before a party, spray her hair with some glitter spray. She will love this!
- Get some cute scarves in different colors and tie one in a do-rag around her head, alternating colors each time she wears one. Simply fold the bandana or scarf into a triangle. Place the straight edge of the triangle on the crown of her head. Take the corners at the end of the straight edge and wrap them around the back of her head. Tie these two pieces into a knot. This is a great way to handle her hair during summer sports.

CHAPTER 2

Bonding over How She Cares for Her Skin

There is nothing more enjoyable than designating fifteen minutes a day to pampering your daughter. Remember when she was a baby? You would give her a bath, rub baby lotion all over her, and she would smell so kissably sweet. Well, you can still give her that attention, but in a more grown-up way. For example, my daughter and I love yummy-smelling body lotions and scrubs, so every day we make her bath or shower a fun experience. She is old enough to shower by herself, so I give her a body scrub to use or sometimes a new shower gel. When she comes out, I wrap her in a warm towel, and she picks out her favorite body lotion. Then I give her a little back massage, and we talk about her day. It just takes a few a minutes, but it gets a dialogue going, and at the same time, I am getting her into the habit of moisturizing her skin each night.

Great skin care starts with you. Teaching your daughter how to wash her face properly and keep her skin healthy and radiant is a great habit that will last a lifetime. Contrary to what many people think, cleansing regimens, creams, and facials are not just for older women. If your daughter is wearing makeup or plays sports, her face needs to be cleansed nightly to remove dirt and oil. If you live in a dry climate or you have dry heat in the winter, moisturizing her face every night before bed is also a great habit to get into.

Unfortunately, puberty can be hard on a young girl. If she has freckles and is self-conscious about them, you have to tell her how beautiful they are and why they make her unique. She may develop pimples, blackheads, and even acne. This chapter will tell you what to do if she gets a few zits after eating junk food or before her period. You will also learn how to prevent and treat acne before it gets out of control.

As a mom, you have to be your daughter's cheerleader and help her do everything possible to feel great about herself. Your daily votes of confidence and affirmation of your daughter will mean the world to her at this vulnerable age. Just remember to keep the compliments honest and not exaggerated. If you overdo it, she will not believe you are being truthful.

In this chapter, I also share with you another great way to spend time with your daughter: giving her an at-home facial. If she has beautiful skin already, this is an excellent way to preserve it. At-home facials are easy to do, and most everything you need is in your refrigerator or at your local drugstore, so it won't cost you a week's pay. It can be a monthly event that includes shopping together for products, taking photos of your day, and even inviting some friends to join the fun. Be a cool mom who puts aside an hour to do this with her daughter. I bet you will enjoy it as much as your daughter does.

Caring for her in this way is an easy way to build communication between the two of you. To share an example from my own life, I help my daughter clean her face each night after she finishes her homework. It gives us a chance to talk about her day, her friends, and anything that may be on her mind. During this private time, she often talks about her feelings and tells me things about her life I might not otherwise know. Before bed, I give her a little facial massage with moisturizer to relax her before sleep. It is amazing how taking an extra ten minutes with her each night makes her feel treasured and special.

Pretty, soft, unblemished skin makes any girl feel and look great. If you teach her great skin care now, I guarantee she will remember it forever. One of my fondest memories is of my mother giving my friend and me cucumber slices for our eyes and yogurt masks when we had a sleepover. I also remember going to my friend Nicole's house and her mother instructing us to clean our faces with St. Ives Apricot Scrub and following it up with the Collage Elastin moisturizer. To this day, I have those products in my bathroom. Girls love to feel grown-up like mom. This chapter will make you a skin care expert with all the know-how and fun activities to make your daughter feel beautiful and glamorous. She and her friends will think you are the coolest mom there is!

The Right Products for the Right Result

Great skin begins with the right products. But there are so many skin care products on the market it is often difficult to know which ones to buy. One basic rule of thumb to remember is that more expensive does not necessarily mean better. If a cream is so expensive that you are afraid for your daughter to use it, what good is it? Products you find at your local drugstore, and even in your own refrigerator, are likely just fine for her unless she has very sensitive skin or a specific skin problem. If you can find organic products with natural ingredients, those are even better.

Further on in this chapter, you'll learn lots of great ways to use fruits, vegetables, and ordinary items from your pantry to cleanse and hydrate the skin.

Many common skin problems can be prevented or treated at home if you implement a good cleansing routine. Other, more severe, problems such as acne need the help of a dermatologist.

When choosing skin care products, particularly for young, sensitive, or pre-pubescent skin, keep in mind the terms *hypoallergenic* and *noncomedogenic*. (In the next chapter, I'll give you more details about noncomedogenic makeup products.) *Hypoallergenic* means the product should not cause an allergic reaction or irritate the skin. *Noncomedogenic* means the product should not clog pores. But be aware there is no industry standard stipulating what makes a product hypoallergenic or noncomedogenic. The FDA does not regulate this. Additionally, a product that claims to be noncomedogenic because it does not clog pores could still irritate the skin if it contains retinol or some other acne-fighting ingredient. As a rule, try to buy fragrance-free products to minimize any possible allergic reaction. Also, test any new product on your daughter's wrist before applying it to her face. Noncomedogenic products are best if your daughter's skin is beginning to show signs of acne, pimples, and blackheads.

Be sure to consult a licensed dermatologist before allowing your daughter to use acne lotions that contain salicylic acid, vitamin A, or retinol because these ingredients can cause burning and irritation. Acne really needs to be treated professionally to avoid scarring of the skin. However, before implementing any treatment for acne, see chapter 7, "Bonding over Nutrition & Fitness," to see if changing her diet clears her acne. Oftentimes, food sensitivities or excessive consumption of greasy foods can be the culprit. If you do feel she needs treatment, see a licensed dermatologist rather than an aesthetician.

I also want to help you understand the difference between soaps and other cleansers. Soaps contain surfactants, or detergents, and are alkaline. They can strip the skin of essential oils and leave it dry and tight. Soap-free cleansers are less alkaline and therefore gentler on the skin. They come in liquids, gels, bars, and creams and usually leave skin feeling less dry than soap does. Products referred to as beauty bars, body cleansers, and face washes are usually soap-free cleansers.

Skin care should be fun for you and your daughter. I consulted with my favorite aesthetician, Ilona Taithy, owner of a European Skin & Hair Salon in New York. She gave me directions for making some wonderful masks in my kitchen from foods almost everyone has in their home. When my daughter's friends come over, the first thing they want to do is make masks, put cucumber slices on their eyes, and have me take pictures of them. We have such a great time, and you will too!

Now, Take Her Shopping!

While I love my daughter, I do not love to spend a fortune on her. With the clothes, the shoes, and all the things in between, it adds up fast. Plus, I think expensive beauty products are a waste of money. With today's emphasis on products free from chemicals and preservatives, most drugstores are stocking their shelves with reasonably priced products containing organic and natural ingredients. In the next section, I have outlined some of my favorite products you can buy at your local drugstore at a low cost. But don't go alone. Tell your daughter you are going on a special shopping trip and invite her to come along and pick out a few things to pamper both of you. Make a list of what you need before you go and have her find the items for you. She will love the attention, and it gives you an opportunity to spend time together while also getting your errands done.

WHAT TO BUY

Here is a list of what you may want to get for your daughter. Pick and choose what suits you and your budget.

Unsterilized Cotton Rolls

Ilona Taithy recommends you do not buy acrylic cotton balls. Instead, buy a roll of acrylic-free, unsterilized absorbent cotton. This is because it takes so many balls of cotton to clean your entire face, and doing so still does not do the job as well as cleaning with a big wad of cotton. A roll of unsterilized cotton will last you three months or more and costs under $6.00, whereas each box of cotton balls will be gone in a month and costs about $4.00.

Cleansers and Moisturizers

There is nothing more fun than perusing the aisles and looking at all the goodies on the shelves. Teach your daughter to read the ingredients on the label to see whether a particular brand is a good product for her. On her list she should have a creamy cleanser, a toner, and a moisturizer with SPF, or sun protection factor.

Ilona Taithy recommends you look for products containing natural ingredients. In addition, here's a list of good ingredients you should concentrate on:

- Apricot, because it has vitamins A, B, and D
- Blueberry, because it protects against dryness
- Peanut oil, because it moisturizes without clogging pores
- Carnation oil, because it reduces signs of aging
- Rice oil, because it is an antioxident and fights free radicals
- Vitamin E oil, because it helps repair skin damage
- Cottonseed oil, because it can be used as a mild surfactant in cleansers
- Honey, because it is a humectant, helping skin to retain water
- Oatmeal, because it helps heal dry, itchy skin
- Corn, because it is a rich emollient
- Fruit acids, because they help exfoliate dead skin
- Natural butters such as coconut and almond butter, because they are emollients

Here's a short list of ingredients that you should avoid:

- Mineral oil if your daughter's skin is oily
- Heavy fragrance, especially for a tween with sensitive skin
- Petroleum
- Hydrogen peroxide

Eye Makeup Remover

I love and recommend buying Neutrogena Makeup Remover Cleansing Towelettes for any tween who insists on wearing eyeliner

Need to Know

Aesthetician—A skin care specialist trained in skin treatment, but who has no medical degree. Usually, these professionals work in salons giving facials or as consultants to dermatologists.

Astringent—A liquid used after a cleanser to remove excess dirt and makeup and restore skin's pH balance. It is used on oily skin to tighten pores. An astringent contains 2 to 5 percent alcohol.

Blackheads—A blackhead appears as a black dot on the surface of the skin when a hair follicle becomes clogged with dirt and oil.

Exfoliant—A grainy product that removes dead skin cells from the skin's surface.

Hypoallergenic—A product that claims it will not irritate the skin.

Noncomedogenic—A product that claims it will not clog pores.

Loofah—An abrasive sponge made out of natural fibers used in the shower to slough dry skin off the body and stimulate circulation.

Pore minimizer—A product formulated to address the appearance of enlarged pores. Minimizers reduce the look of enlarged pores and refine skin texture so makeup can go on smoothly. These products are more for older tweens after puberty.

Soap—A product composed of animal or vegetable fat and an alkaline material (about pH 13). The soap pulls the fatty acids and the dirt attached to them from the skin. Soap comes in bar and liquid form.

Soap-free cleanser—A skin-cleaning product that differs from soap in that it is nonalkaline (pH 6 or 7), or balanced.

SPF—A number that indicates the amount of protection against the sun's rays given by a sunscreen.

Toner—A liquid used after applying cleanser to remove excess dirt and makeup and to restore the skin's pH balance. Toners are best for normal to dry skin because they usually contain no alcohol.

and mascara. These towelettes are very soft and gentle and even re-move waterproof mascara. You could also look for liquid eye makeup remover, which should be applied with a piece of cotton.

Skin Care for the Face

A girl's complexion is determined by heredity, diet, how much water she drinks, and her daily skin care regimen. It is essential that your daughter keep her face clean and always moisturized, but you must first determine her skin type to know how best to approach her complexion maintenance. On the facing page is a fun activity for the two of you that will help you figure out her skin type. Go to the refrigerator and get a lemon, an orange, and an apple. Then, one at a time, hold each one up to her face to determine her skin type.

Now that you know what your daughter's skin type is, it's time to get that pretty, young skin looking fabulous. Let's start by help-ing her learn the basics of caring for her skin properly.

CLEANSING ROUTINE

You and your daughter should follow a nightly routine of washing and moisturizing your faces. Make it a part of her bedtime routine right before she brushes her teeth.

Quick Clean

Have her wash with a milky cleanser or a cleansing cloth. My favorite cleanser is Mario Badescu Cleansing Milk with Carna-tion & Rice Oil available at www.mariobadescu.com. It is super gentle and made with great ingredients.

What's Her Skin Type?

Is she a lemon?

Dry skin has fine pores and looks like the skin of a lemon. It feels dry and smooth to the touch. It can often get flaky around the mouth and nose.

Is she an apple?

Normal skin has no visible pores and looks like the skin of an apple. It is smooth to the touch.

Is she an orange?

Oily skin has large open pores and looks like the skin of an orange. Oily skin often looks shiny—very shiny—and feels greasy to the touch.

Combination skin has dry patches and oily areas.

Acne-prone skin tends to develop blackheads, white heads, cysts, and clusters of pimples.

Sensitive skin reacts to irritants. It can get itchy and red when the wrong products are used.

My Favorite Cleansing Routine
For this routine, you need:

- Cotton from the cotton roll, not cotton balls
- Milky cleanser
- Eye makeup remover (if she wears eye makeup)
- Toner or astringent for oily skin

First, have your daughter break off a piece of cotton the size of her palm. Have her moisten the cotton under the faucet and form it into a cheek-size pad by folding down the edges. When she has a nice pad, she can squeeze out the excess water. Next, have her pour a milky cleanser on the cotton and wipe her entire face gently to remove dirt and makeup. For stubborn eye makeup, she can use an eye makeup remover. Teach her to be extra gentle around the eye area, never pulling or rubbing that sensitive skin. Finally, have her turn the cotton pad over, pour toner or astringent onto that clean side, and remove the excess dirt.

CREAM UP!
Night cream for a ten-year-old? Well, not your night cream. But moisturizing before bed can never start too young. Most sun damage occurs before age eighteen. The younger your girl starts the creams, the longer she'll go before needing fillers like Botox and Restylane! Every morning and night she must use a moisturizer appropriate for her skin type. However, for oily skin, I would stick to an oil-free moisturizer. For acne-prone skin, it is not necessary to moisturize. I also think it is never too early to use a gentle eye cream around the eyes.

MOISTURIZE AND NOURISH FROM THE INSIDE

You and your daughter have to drink as much water as you can. Avoid soda, juice, juice drinks, or powdered drinks. A good rule of thumb is the following:

> Drink half your weight in ounces each day.
> Example: 120 pounds ÷ 2 = 60 ounces of water per day.

Just as with drinking enough water each day, diet makes or breaks the skin. Grease in her mouth means grease on her face! If your daughter has oily skin, avoid chips, fast foods, or excess sugars. And in general, you should both be eating lots of foods with essential nutrients for healthy skin. (See chapter 7, "Bonding over Nutrition & Fitness," for suggestions on what to eat for great skin.)

Now that you know the basics, you're ready to help your daughter establish healthy skin care habits. Read on to discover the ins and outs of caring for specific skin types.

Normal to Dry Facial Skin

If your daughter has beautiful skin and is not prone to breakouts, blemishes, or allergic reactions, her skin care regimen can be fairly simple. Your goal is to keep her skin cleansed and well hydrated. If her skin looks dull and flaky, she can use a gentle scrub once per week to remove dead skin cells. Also, make sure she is eating healthy fresh food and sleeping at least nine hours per night. That means going to bed no later than 9:30 PM and up at 7:00 AM.

CLEANSE

Clean off dirt and makeup each night before bed with a soap-free cleanser or milky cleanser. Ideally, have her follow the "My Favorite Cleansing Routine" given in the earlier section called "Skin Care for the Face." After using the milky cleanser, apply an alcohol-free toner—*not* an astringent.

MOISTURIZE

Moisturizing normal to dry facial skin keeps it soft and supple. It is a great habit for your daughter to get into especially as she gets older.

- Night: Before bed, apply a light moisturizer to entire face.
- Morning: Each morning, use a light moisturizer with an SPF. For blemishes or unevenly colored skin, tinted moisturizers can give the face a nice even glow.
- Summer: In the summer, when skin is oilier, use lighter moisturizers containing lots of water.
- Winter: In the winter, use creamier products to protect against cold weather dryness. Avoid watery products, which will freeze on the skin.

EXFOLIATE

It is not necessary to exfoliate the face before puberty. Once a girl enters puberty, however, Ilona Taithy recommends that she exfoliate with a gentle scrub once per week.

Oily and Combination Facial Skin

Look at your daughter. Do her nose and forehead have a shine soon after she washes her face? Girls with oily or combination skin often wash their faces day and night with strong soaps and astringents, trying to get rid of the oil. I'll bet you didn't know that this is the worst thing they can do! It makes the oil glands work overtime to replace the oils the girls wash away. The trick to managing oily skin is to calm down the glands so they produce less oil.

It is not always necessary to consult a dermatologist for treating oily or combination skin. First, try the following routine for a few weeks to see if you can get her skin looking better. Also see chapter 7, "Bonding over Nutrition & Fitness," to make sure she is eating the best diet for her skin. Also make sure she is sleeping at least nine hours per night.

If you are not happy with how her skin is looking, seek the advice of a licensed aesthetician, who will then try to help her with her skin care regimen. Find somebody who works with natural products. Do not go to somebody in the back of a nail salon. If your daughter's skin is not as you would like it within three to six months, see a dermatologist.

CLEANSE

In the morning, she should clean skin with an oil-free, soap-free cleanser. Instead of using products with strong ingredients like alcohol or benzol peroxide that can irritate her skin, suggest that she pat shiny areas with damp cotton throughout the day to remove the surface oil without drying out the skin. This will prevent the oil glands from getting a message that the skin is dry, so they will not produce more oil.

At night, cleanse skin with an oil-free, soap-free cleanser. Remove excess dirt and oil with a piece of cotton saturated with a toner. Grape juice or grapefruit juice can be used as a toner as well. Rinse with a splash of water.

MOISTURIZE

In the morning and at night—particularly in the winter—after washing the face, apply an oil-free moisturizer such as Clean & Clear Morning Burst Morning Glow. During the summer months no moisturizer is necessary.

EXFOLIATE

After puberty, your daughter can use a gentle scrub to clean her face once per week if she has dry patches on her face.

Acne-Prone Facial Skin

Acids in normal skin fight bacteria and germs. Acne-prone skin lacks natural germ-fighting acids. The skin does not have adequate protection, which allows infections to form clusters of pimples and blackheads. I caution you not to freak out at the first sign of breakouts and assume it is acne. It could just be a surge in her hormones or too much junk food. If the breakout does not clear within two weeks then take her to a dermatologist to find out what is really going on.

It is unusual for a girl to have serious acne until she is a teenager. If you had acne when you were younger and you see the signs of it appearing on your daughter, do not treat it at home. See a dermatologist. Most acne is treatable with the help of a dermatologist. If left untreated, the acne could irritate your daughter to the point of her picking at the skin with dirty fingers, which can aggravate the acne and even scar the skin.

DR. FRIEDMAN-KIEN'S ACNE ADVICE

Dr. Friedman-Kien is a dermatologist at New York University's medical center and a professor of dermatology and microbiology. I asked him to share what he considers the essential facts for mothers and their daughters to know about acne:

- Acne is caused by increased activity of the sebaceous glands, which is often due to hormonal changes at puberty, heredity, and greasy foods, as well as other unknown causes.
- If acne is not treated properly, it can leave deformative scarring that is very difficult to get rid of later in life.
- Acne usually occurs in girls between the ages of eleven and fourteen.
- A board-certified dermatologist should be consulted to treat acne.
- A dermatologist will typically treat acne with a topical ointment. If acne is more severe, the dermatologist may prescribe an oral antibiotic to treat the problem. However, it is best in young girls to start with the milder treatments to see if the skin responds.
- An over-the-counter acne wash is fine for daily cleansing.
- Moisturizers should be avoided because skin is already overproducing oil.

CLEANSE

In the morning and at night, clean skin with an oil-free acne cleanser recommended by your daughter's dermatologist. I like Neutrogena Oil-Free Acne Wash. Once per week spread an acne mask (prescribed by a dermatologist or recommended by a skin specialist) on face and throat and let it sit for twenty minutes. Remove mask with warm water. The mask will deep clean and tighten pores.

MOISTURIZE

Do not moisturize acne-prone skin.

EXFOLIATE

Avoid facial scrubs especially if she is using acne medication. The scrub could aggravate the skin, which may be more sensitive due to the strong ingredients from the acne products.

Sensitive Facial Skin

If your daughter has freckles and the skin on her face gets irritated easily, the products she uses are extremely important. For more than forty years, Mario Badescu Skin Care Salon in New York has been known for personalized skin care treatments and products. The aestheticians at Mario Badescu recommend you try to figure out exactly what irritates her skin and avoid those ingredients. You can't go wrong, in the meantime, by always choosing and using alchohol-free, fragrance-free, hypoallergenic products. To be safe, test the product on your daughter's wrist twenty-four hours before she plans on applying it to her face and watch for any reaction. If she reacts to every product she tries, I would recommend cleansing her skin with yogurt instead of a cleanser and moisturizing with coconut oil.

CLEANSE

Clean off dirt and makeup each night before bed with a milky cleanser or Cetaphil using "My Favorite Cleansing Routine." To avoid irritation, I would not use a toner.

MOISTURIZE

In the morning and again at night before bed, have your daughter apply a creamy moisturizer all over her face. My daughter's skin is very sensitive, so I like her to use products such as Aveeno, Aquaphor, or Eucerin. Always avoid the areas around the eyes.

EXFOLIATE

Do not exfoliate sensitive skin. It could cause irritation and redness.

Dealing with Blackheads and Pimples

There is no exception to the following rule: To remove blackheads, go to a salon and have a professional give your daughter a facial. Blackheads are follicles filled with dead skin and sebum. They are too deep to remove at home. You will scar your daughter's skin if you try to do it yourself.

Dr. Friedman-Kien does not recommend squeezing a pimple because any type of squeezing can scar the skin. It is okay to put a topical ointment such as Bremenn Emergency Zit Stick on a pimple to dry it up, or you can run hot water over a tissue or clean washcloth and press it against the pimple. Do this a few times a day. The pimple will spontaneously burst or resolve itself internally.

MORE TIPS ON HOW TO TREAT PIMPLES

If the pimple is underneath the skin, cosmetologist Ilona Taithy recommends taking half of a strawberry and rubbing it on the pimple to dry it up. If the pimple comes to a whitehead and bursts, clean the area with tea tree oil or an antibacterial ointment.

Makeup artist Maria Maio suggests you mash up a baby aspirin and mix it with a saline solution or clean water to make a paste. Dab the paste on the pimple before bed to dry it up.

Popping a Pimple

While I do not think you should pop your daughter's pimples, I know many people do it. Keep in mind you could scar her skin. However, if you are going to do it anyway, you should know how they do it in the salons.

Remember only pop it if it has a white cap on it. To get a white cap, you need to apply a topical pimple cream and leave it on for at least twelve hours. Only do this before bed, not before she goes to school. It will look worse before it looks better.

1. Have her take a hot shower for ten minutes to open pores.
2. After the shower, wrap clean cotton around your two index fingers. Dip covered fingers in tea tree oil, toner, or astringent. Squeeze out excess liquid.
3. Put each finger at the base of the pimple. Squeeze the base, pushing fingers upwards until all the white pus comes out.

4. Stop squeezing and clean the area with cotton and astringent.

5. Stop the blood with a small piece of cotton.

6. If she must go out, do not use make-up for at least half an hour.

At-Home Facials

Facials are a great way for you and your daughter to spend time together having fun and relaxing. You can give a facial to your daughter and even her friends during a sleepover. I have included simple recipes for making your own masks to use during an at-home facial. The more things you can make in your kitchen, the bigger the fun. Can you imagine anything better than making your own beauty products in the kitchen and then smearing it on your face? Your daughter will absolutely love this!

To get started with the facial, lay out everything you will need on a table:

- Milky cleanser
- Toner or astringent
- Light moisturizer
- Mask (make one of the recipes that follow to have handy when you are ready for it)
- Cotton
- Lip balm
- Cold cucumber slices for the eyes

Your tween should wear a robe, a towel, or

zip-up sweatshirt that can easily expose her neck and shoulders. Push her hair off her face with a headband. Wash your hands and scrub underneath your fingernails before touching her face.

STEAM AND CLEANSE

Mario Badescu Skin Care Salon recommends you use steam to relax the pores for the first step in the facial. The steam softens the skin's surface and increases circulation to the face to facilitate the removal of dead skin and dirt later on. Here is the step-by-step process they suggest following:

1. Boil a pot of water and, if you have it, add a chamomile tea bag. You can also experiment and use different teas, like mint and strawberry. Put the boiling water in an open pot since your daughter will be breathing in the steam from the tea. Carefully place the pot on a surface where it will not spill.

2. Let the tea bag steep in the boiled water for five minutes. While the tea is brewing, do "My Favorite Cleansing Routine" (in the "Skin Care for the Face" section earlier in this chapter) on your daughter to clean her skin.

3. Once her skin is clean, place a towel over both her head and the pot as she leans forward over it. Have her inhale the steam from the tea for five to ten minutes. The towel keeps the steam from escaping and concentrates it on her face. If the steam feels too hot, she should not lean in as closely.

4. Remove the towel. Her face should be pink and covered with perspiration. Put the tea aside (it can be used for someone else if reheated).

5. Splash some cold water on her face, and gently pat her skin dry with a washcloth.

FACIAL MASSAGE

The facial massage step in a facial increases blood circulation to the face and feels wonderful. Follow these steps for best results:

1. Use a moisturizer appropriate for your daughter's skin type. (If your daughter has oily skin you can use an oil-free moisturizer and then clean it off with a damp piece of cotton when you are done, or you do not have to use a cream at all.) It should be a light cream that moves easily on the face. With your fingers, dab the cream on both sides of the neck, cheeks, nose, and forehead.

2. Using the cushions of the middle and ring fingers, alternate upward strokes, gently lifting the skin without pulling it.

3. Do two sets of ten strokes on the neck, the right cheek, the left cheek, and finally the forehead. You should always use the same number of strokes and the same rhythm for a more relaxing, even massage.

4. With both thumbs, rub the chin in circles. The right thumb goes clockwise and the left thumb goes counterclockwise.

5. With the tips of the fingers, lightly massage both cheeks simultaneously in circular movements. Make ten complete circles.

6. Alternate upward strokes with both hands on the forehead. Start in the middle with two sets of ten strokes. Do the same on the right side of the forehead, the left side, and then the middle again.

7. Gently press on the temples. Applying slight pressure, take the two middle fingers and press along the eyebrows from the inner corners to the outer corners. Press on the temples again. Repeat five times. The slower you do this, the better it feels.

THE MASK

The most fun part about an at-home facial is making a mask from ingredients in your kitchen. Some masks tighten pores, others deep clean, and there are even masks to firm the skin. See the section called "Mask Recipes" and make the mask appropriate for her skin type.

Here are the steps for applying the mask:

1. Place the cucumber slices over her eyes.
2. Apply the mask to the whole face with your fingers. Leave it on until it dries, about ten to twenty minutes.
3. Remove the cucumber slices.
4. Clean off the mask with some moist cotton or have her go to the sink to rinse it off her face.

TONING AND MOISTURIZING

1. Clean off mask residue with a piece of cotton saturated with toner.
2. Spread a thin layer of a light moisturizer.
3. With a cotton swab, spread a lip balm over her lips.

After you have finished her facial, her skin should look great. Now, let her give you a facial. You will love it too!

MASK RECIPES

Ilona Taithy gave me the following mask recipes. Use the recipes for your at-home facial or even once a week for fun. Because the ingredients are all natural, they are safe and gentle for all skin types.

Egg and Yogurt Mask

The egg and yogurt mask firms the skin while adding softness. This is great for you too!

You will need

    2 eggs whites

    2 tablespoons of plain yogurt (do not use flavored yogurt!) or sour cream

Directions

1. Beat egg whites in a bowl until frothy.
2. Add 2 tablespoons of yogurt or sour cream. Stir thoroughly.

Blueberry Soy Hydrating Mask

You will need

    10 blueberries

    ½ teaspoon of soymilk

Directions

1. Crush the blueberries in a bowl. Mash them well.
2. Add soy milk and mix well.

Carrot Honey Nourishing Mask

You will need

    1/3 cup of carrot juice

    The pulp of half an orange

    1 teaspoon honey

Directions

Mix the carrot juice, the orange pulp, and the honey until smooth.

Honey Oatmeal Mask (Mario Badescu Skin Care Salon recommends this particular mask to absorb oil and calm the skin.)

You will need

> ½ cup dry old-fashioned oatmeal
>
> ¼ avocado
>
> 1 teaspoon honey
>
> 1 tablespoon olive oil

Directions

> 1. In a bowl, mix the honey, olive oil, and avocado.
> 2. Add in the oatmeal and mix thoroughly.

If you prefer to buy a mask, buy a hydrating herbal mask for dry to normal skin and a clay-based mask for oily and combination and acne-prone skin. Go to www.mariobadescu.com and choose a mask for your daughter's skin type. They are all really wonderful.

Skin Care for the Body

Skin care starts in your shower. This is where your daughter washes and exfoliates her body. Our children's lives have become so hectic with hours of homework, after-school sports, and a whole host of extracurricular activities. While we need to inspire them to work hard, it is also important to teach them how to relax so they can balance the pressures of daily life. The bath or shower is the one place your daughter can take a deep breath, relax, and shut out the world. Encourage her to take this time for herself to care for her skin and relax her mind. (See chapter 8, "Bonding over Aromatherapy to Feel Beautiful," on how to add essential oils to the experience.)

SCRUBS

While a scrub is not a must-have, girls do love the feeling of using them. It makes home feel like a spa. I do not recommend using a scrub very often on young skin. Children's skin is fragile, so you want to make sure anything you use is gentle. If you want to try a scrub on her body, either buy one designed for the face (because it will not be too harsh) or make your own using one of the following recipes. Have her use the scrub to exfoliate after she washes her body in the shower.

SCRUB RECIPES

A fun activity you can do together is to make your own scrubs. The following scrubs feel great and leave skin soft and supple.

Oatmeal Yogurt Scrub

This scrub is gentle enough to be used on the face.

You will need

    1 cup of dry old-fashioned oatmeal flakes

    1 cup sour cream or plain yogurt.

Directions

Mix the oatmeal with the sour cream or yogurt. In the shower or over the sink, gently have her scrub her face with the mixture.

Brown Sugar Scrub

The brown sugar scrub is wonderful to use all over the body. I especially like it when I give my daughter an at-home pedicure.

You will need

    ½ cup of brown sugar

    2 tablespoons of almond oil or olive oil

5 drops of honey

3 to 5 drops of your favorite essential oil (optional)

Directions

Mix ingredients thoroughly in a glass bowl. In the shower, she can scrub her whole body with the mixture.

Tropical Fruit and Sugar Scrub

You will need

½ cup of white sugar

3 tablespoons of coconut milk or coconut oil

3 tablespoons of almond oil, jojoba oil, or olive oil

½ cup of fresh papaya

Directions

1. Mix the sugar and all the oils.
2. Puree fruit in a blender or food processor.
3. Add the pureed fruit to the sugar mixture.

In the shower, she can gently scrub her whole body with the mixture.

SHOWERS AND BATHS

The first rule of skin care in the shower is *do not* share products or tools that directly touch the skin! I'm not talking about toothpaste and shampoo; I'm talking about razors, bar soaps, loofahs, and towels. If a member of the family has a skin problem, sharing items that directly touch the skin is a great way to pass it on to everyone else. Towels spread warts, molluscum, and other skin viruses. So, assuming no one is sharing products or tools that directly touch the skin, here are my tips:

- Cool It Down: If your daughter feels tired after her shower, she should take a shorter, cooler shower. Long, hot showers dehydrate the skin and can leave her feeling tired.

- No More Bars: Soap-free liquid cleansers instead of bar soaps are great because they do not dry out the skin the way many traditional bar soaps do. And as I mentioned earlier, these cleansers are more sanitary, especially if other family members use the same tub or shower.

- Be Sensitive: If your daughter's skin is ultrasensitive, use Cetaphil cleanser or try a homemade body wash in place of a liquid cleanser. Ilona Taithy recommends you mix in a blender a ripe green apple, a ripe pear, and a cup of plain yogurt and use the mixture in place of soap in the shower.

- Exfoliate: Encourage your daughter to exfoliate once per month with a scrub. Either use a scrub directly on the skin or apply soap to a loofah and scrub areas prone to dry skin or even cellulite. Remind her to avoid sensitive places like her face, neck, and breasts.

- Pat, Don't Rub: She should not rub her skin with a towel to dry it; patting dry avoids stripping the skin of moisture. A terry-cloth robe instead of a towel is a good choice because it dries her body while she wears it. Wash her towels or terry-cloth robe at least once per week. When washing towels, don't use fabric softener, which will coat the towel, making it less absorbent.

- Moisturize: She should moisturize immediately after she showers, preferably before the skin is completely dry. Baby oil or coconut oil is a great, inexpensive moisturizer that she can rub all over damp skin to lock in moisture. And you can purchase oils that have added vitamin E to support the health of the skin. Cocoa butter is also great to use on breasts, buttocks, and thighs to prevent stretch marks as her body develops during puberty.

Cellulite

Those cottage cheese–like dimples you find on the butt, thighs, stomach, around the knees, and sometimes on the arms are known as cellulite. Cellulite is fat that is trapped in pockets formed in the connective tissue that lies beneath the skin. This connective tissue tethers the skin to other tissues beneath the skin (such as muscle) at certain points, creating chambers or pockets. Cellulite is a problem for women far more often than it is for men because the connective tissue in women is structured very differently from the connective tissue in men. In men, those pockets don't typically form.

When we hit puberty, the connective tissue begins to contract and stiffen. As fat increases in certain areas, it pushes into the pockets and pushes out against the skin. At the same time, the connective tissue is pulling the skin in at certain points. And so bumps and lumps are created.

Unfortunately, if you have it, your daughter is likely to have it too, as it is hereditary (based on skin type and structure). And once you have it, it takes some work to minimize it. You have to reduce the amount of fat beneath the skin, improve the health of the skin, and improve the flexibility and suppleness of the connective tissue. If you have cellulite and your daughter does not, I believe you can help her avoid it. Here are some tips for minimizing cellulite and for helping your daughter develop good habits that will limit her cellulite problems in the future:

- Diet: Eat a healthy diet full of whole foods to keep toxins from building up. Also, eat lots of foods that contain the essential nutrients necessary for healthy skin (see chapter 7, "Bonding over Nutrition & Fitness"). Finally, help her eat as many natural, organic, or hormone-free foods as possible. Girls today are going through puberty earlier due in part to the hormones present in the foods they eat. The earlier she goes through puberty, the sooner her connective tissues will become more rigid and cause cellulite to appear.

- Exercise: Regular exercise not only helps prevent the buildup of fat but also increases circulation to the skin and the connective tissue, making them stronger, healthier, and more supple. Dance, cheerleading, soccer, field hockey, softball, track, lacrosse, basketball, exercising with videos, yoga, swimming, walking, and biking all get the blood pumping, which leads to better circulation and better skin health.

- Massage: Applying cellulite cream promotes massage, which increases circulation. I think they are expensive and are really no better than massaging the body with an inexpensive moisturizer. The best option I have found is to have your daughter use a loofah a few times a week to bring circulation to problem areas. A loofah is inexpensive and really works well. After showering, massage problem areas with a moisturizer or baby oil.

Sun Care

Save your daughter's beautiful skin from wrinkles and skin cancer. Most sun damage is done before age eighteen, so you have the power to prevent it. Ilona Taithy encourages mothers to educate their daughters about sun protection. Skin is like a computer and it remembers every sunburn. Be sure she uses a lotion with an SPF before going in the sun. Ilona does not recommend an SPF higher than 30 because the chemical content is very high. However, dermatologist Dr. Friedman-Kien believes children should use SPF 50 that fights UVA and UVB rays to avoid premature aging and prevent skin cancer.

The biggest dilemma we mothers face is chemicals versus sun protection. The higher the SPF, the higher the chemical content, but the better the protection. This is really a personal decision you will have to make. Whichever SPF you choose, keep reapplying the sunscreen so your girl's skin does not burn. If she does burn, hydrate and soothe the skin with an aloe vera gel.

The following section contains some sunscreen facts to help your daughter build good habits early.

SUNSCREEN

SPF, remember, stands for "sun protection factor." *In theory*, the SPF multiplies your skin's natural ability to protect itself from solar energy, or ultraviolet (UV) radiation. So, if you customarily burn in ten minutes, an SPF 15 could, *in theory*, protect the skin for 150 minutes. *But*, your exposure or reaction to UV radiation changes based on many factors, so it's safe to say that the actual protection will not last that long. Some factors that influence how long your daughter's skin is protected include:

- The time of day
- Her skin type
- The condition of her skin
- How much sunscreen you rubbed on her and how much her skin absorbed
- How much she is sweating or how much time she is spending in water

Products that claim to protect skin for six hours may *stay* on the skin for six hours but don't necessarily *protect* for six hours. If the product has an SPF of only 15 and her skin burns in ten minutes, she will still likely burn after two hours. You just may not have to reapply the sunscreen during those first two hours. I advise you to warn your daughter not to go out into the sun with an SPF lower than 15. Ideally, she should use SPF 30 or above if she will be in the sun all day. She should reapply sunscreen every two hours, sooner if she will be swimming. She should apply the sunscreen thirty minutes before sun exposure.

Most sunscreens protect against UVB radiation. According to Dr. Friedman-Kien, however, the UV radiation most often associated with cancer due to sun damage is UVA radiation. Not all sunscreens offer UVA protection so choose your sunscreen carefully. Sunscreens that offer the best UVA protection usually contain zinc oxide, avobenzone, and ecamsule. The best sunscreens are PABA free, noncomedogenic, and fragrance free. They are less likely to cause rashes, irritations, and breakouts.

SUNLESS TANNING

Before she considers using any tanning products, have your daughter think about makeup. She can get that sun-kissed look on her face by using makeup. Find a bronzer that matches her skin tone when she is tan. Apply it to her upper cheekbones, temples, forehead, the tip of her nose, and chin. Basically, put bronzer on all the places the sun would naturally hit.

If makeup isn't going to cut it, try some of the following options.

Self-Tanners

Self-tanners are a better alternative than baking in the sun, but they do contain many chemicals. Although they give you a healthy tan without risk of skin cancer and premature aging, I would use them sparingly.

Self-tanners dye the top layer of skin. The first application usually gives you a light color, and the second application looks darker. They come in sprays and lotions or creams.

Caution: Always test the self-tanner on her arm before applying it to the body to check color and for a possible allergic reaction.

To apply a self-tanning spray, follow these steps:

1. Exfoliate the skin with a loofah in the shower. After the shower, apply a light moisturizer and let it sit for a couple of minutes. Blot the excess off with a towel.
2. Mist the tanning spray all over the body, but don't rub it in.

3. After fifteen minutes, mist the spray all over the body again and rub it in evenly over the skin. Let it dry. Use a sponge to smooth the spray into creases.
4. Wash hands to avoid tanning palms and fingernails.

To apply self-tanning creams, follow these steps:

1. Scrub the skin with a loofah to get rid of the dead surface skin.
2. Mix the self-tanner with a little water in the palm of the hand; this will give a more even application and avoid spottiness.
3. Spread the cream as evenly as possible over the skin and let it absorb thoroughly before putting on clothing.
4. Wash hands to avoid tanning palms and fingernails.

A Note About Tanning Salons
Tanning salons, like the sun, give you color by using harmful UV rays. The short-term gains are not worth it. If you want your girl to have beautiful skin now, as well as twenty years from now, keep her out of the salons.

Skin Discoloration

I could not end a chapter on skin care without mentioning birthmarks such as raspberries and red wine stains, as well as other birth-related skin discolorations. Dr. Friedman-Kien sees many patients who were born with a raspberry-colored or a red wine stain on the face. Naturally, this is upsetting to any parent as well as to the child. Often parents try to treat the stain aggressively with radiation and lasers. Dr. Friedman-Kien recommends you cover the spots with Dermablend brand coverage or corrective cosmetics. Go to the counter of a department store and have them match the skin tone on your daughter's face. This can help her feel better about her appearance when she goes to school. He also has seen several cases where the mark gets smaller or fades with the onset of puberty. Seek the advice of a reputable dermatologist to find out what the best option is for your daughter.

* * *

While this chapter may seem overwhelming at first, start with something easy. After your daughter's next shower, tell her to put baby oil all over her skin. Once she gets into that habit, have her apply moisturizer to her face each morning before school and every night before bed. Next, embark on the cleansing. Start with the "Quick Clean" described earlier, and then pick a day to give each other the at-home facial and try the "My Favorite Cleansing Routine." Step-by-step, caring for her skin will become second nature. If you do it with her, you may also find you enjoy caring for your own skin in the same way.

Bonding Activities

- Make your own body scrubs or masks with a few simple ingredients from the kitchen. Try the recipes in this book and invent your own.

- Go shopping for new skin care products.
- Do at-home facials for your daughter and her best friend. Take photographs each step of the way and make a scrapbook labeled "My Very First Facial!" Make a video of your day and edit it together with her favorite music.
- Give your daughter a facial massage or back rub before bedtime.
- Do the "My Favorite Cleansing Routine" together.

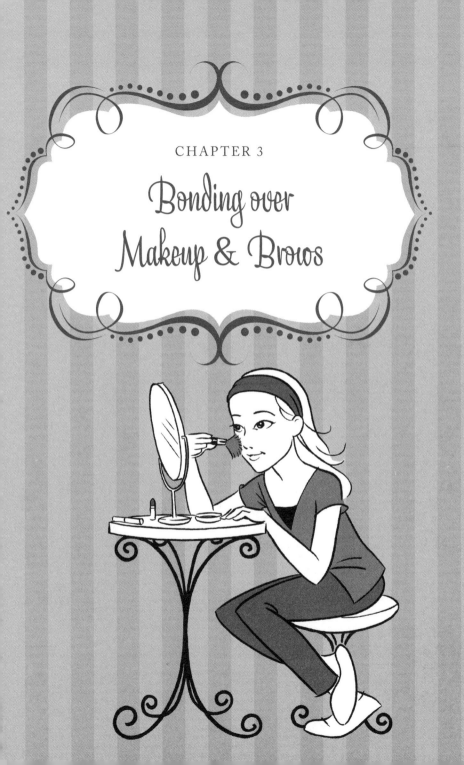

CHAPTER 3

Bonding over Makeup & Brows

Your beautiful, fresh-faced little girl comes out of the bathroom wearing black eyeliner inside her lower lash line and red lipstick. She thinks she looks fabulous. You think she looks like a streetwalker. What do you do? After all, little girls should not wear makeup, right? There is plenty of time for that when she gets into high school . . . or college . . . or her first job. Your daughter is going to put up a big fight because everyone at her school is wearing eye makeup and lipstick. My advice to you: try to embrace the moment and find a compromise that feels appropriate to you both. Most importantly, stay calm and don't make it into a bigger deal than it has to be.

Depending on your daughter's age, makeup may or may not be something you include in your comfort zone for her, especially if you do not wear much makeup yourself. First, try to understand why she wants to wear makeup and then decide how much is appropriate at her particular age. Friends can influence girls tremendously. If all of your tween's friends are wearing eyeliner, she may want to wear it too. But her friends are not her mother—*you* are. So you have the difficult job of deciding when it is okay for her to wear eyeliner. If you are really opposed to makeup in general, agreeing to let your daughter wear lip gloss is always a good compromise. It makes her feel grown up, but she can still look her age. A natural-looking blush can also make her feel like she is made up, but it really just makes her look sun-kissed. Eye makeup inevitably makes girls look older and more provocative than their years, particularly if it is applied heavily. A good solution to the eyeliner issue is to buy a brown pencil and show your daughter how to lightly apply it to enhance the shape of her eye. This way she is wearing makeup, but it looks soft and natural instead of vampish. Another compromise could be to have her do chores around the house to earn makeup money, but maintain your right as the mother to stipulate when she can and cannot wear it.

If you say your daughter is absolutely too young to wear makeup, be aware that she might use other girls' makeup when she gets to school. This is how many girls get eye infections and catch colds. A better solution, I think, is to take the time to educate yourself on makeup application and then show her how to do it. If and when you decide to allow your preteen or teen to wear makeup, you'll have lots of fun taking her shopping and teaching her how to put it on properly to enhance her beauty. This is one opportunity to have a great time together while still maintaining some control over your daughter's appearance.

I believe it is always important to work on inner beauty. However, sometimes it is difficult for a tween to think about such things if she feels her outward appearance is not attractive. In this context, makeup can be a wonderful problem solver. If she has a blemish or a large birthmark on her face, concealer can hide it. If she has a large nose but beautiful eyes, mascara and eyeliner can draw attention to her eyes and thus make her nose seem less important. While makeup is not the answer to all of your daughter's confidence woes, it can give her a great boost.

In this chapter, I'll offer great techniques to apply makeup in three minutes, instructions for applying a more complete makeup, and everything you need to know to create the perfect brow shape. I'll also give you a comprehensive overview of what products are out there and how to use them. Many different types of makeup are on the market, but depending on your daughter's age, some types will not be appropriate. So, pick and choose what you need and have fun shopping.

Is My Daughter Ready for Makeup?

Little girls love to play with makeup as soon as they can get their little fingers into a cosmetic bag. When they are eight, nine, and ten, they usually just want to put on some lip gloss to feel good and to play with something sparkly and shiny. From ages eleven to thirteen, makeup becomes more about being attractive and trying to fit in and be cool. Each mom will face the makeup question at different times depending on her daughter's personality, friends, school, cultural influences, and activities. If you are the mom of the younger tween, try not to make a big deal about wearing makeup. Buy your daughter lip gloss in a few different shades and let her play with it. If you have an older tween, the compromise begins with her respecting the following makeup rules.

MAKEUP RULES

When talking about makeup with your daughter, you have a great opportunity to enforce good health and beauty habits. If she thinks she's ready to wear makeup, tell her it will mean she has to agree to the following rules:

1. She must try to sleep nine hours each night. She can't stay up all night and use concealer the next day to cover dark circles under her eyes.

2. She must remove the makeup every night before she goes to bed.

3. She cannot buy products with too much fragrance (particularly if she has sensitive or allergy-prone skin).

4. She must learn to apply makeup gently, especially around the eyes and nose.

5. She may not share makeup with her friends.

6. She should apply a light moisturizer with an SPF before applying makeup.

7. She should use oil-free, noncomedogenic (i.e., it doesn't block pores) makeup on oily and acne-prone skin.

8. She must keep her makeup and makeup brushes clean and tidy. Makeup left all over the bathroom counter is not acceptable.

9. She must be responsible about her makeup. It is expensive to replace so she must earn it through chores at home or any way you see fit and also take care not to lose it.

10. Her makeup has to be appropriate to her age and where she is going. She cannot wear makeup if she going to overdo it and make herself appear sixteen when she is only twelve.

Finding the Right Makeup

Now that you've gotten used to the idea of your daughter wearing makeup, it's time to enjoy this new chapter in your lives. Tell her you need a new lipstick and pick a day when you both can go to your local department store at the mall. Go up to a makeup counter that targets a younger audience and ask the saleswoman to help you choose makeup for your tween. Celebrity makeup artist Maria Maio suggests you have your daughter pick out a lipstick for you and then you will get to pick out a lip gloss for her.

Have the makeup specialist teach you both how to properly apply makeup so that it looks natural and pretty. You can buy a few things you like or give your daughter a lesson in shopping by suggesting you buy the less expensive versions of products you like in the drugstore. She will love that you are spending time focusing on her appearance. If you are working full time and need to bond with your daughter, what better way than a trip to the mall on your day off to buy makeup!

FOUNDATION AND TINTED MOISTURIZER

Imagine you are painting your room in different colors. First you must plaster the damaged areas and then apply a primer to make the walls one uniform tone before you apply the colored paint.

Foundation and tinted moisturizer are like the primer. They even the skin tone so you have a uniform base from which to work. The trick comes in finding the right color. We've all seen teens with distinct lines on their jaws marking where their foundation ends and their natural skin color begins. Tweens rarely need the kind of coverage that their moms do. Therefore, I would not recommend using a foundation unless your daughter is doing a photo shoot where camera lights are heavy. Laura Geller of Laura Geller Makeup recommends you opt for a tinted moisturizer—a light liquid formula with just a hint of color—that matches her skin tone. This is only applicable to an older tween or if you really feel her skin is uneven and blotchy. If you can find a tinted moisturizer with an SPF, it will actually protect her skin from the sun.

Foundation comes in many forms. For more coverage than a tinted moisturizer provides, you can find whipped or mousse foundations, which are simply liquid foundations whipped with air so that they go on more smoothly. Traditional liquid foundations need to be really well blended into the face and neck with the fingers or a sponge. Cream-to-powder foundations are applied like a liquid, but they look like a powder after they dry; they are especially good for oily skin because they control shine. Finally, there are mineral foundations; I would recommend these for sensitive skin because there are fewer ingredients that could irritate the skin or cause the face to break out.

If you feel your daughter needs a foundation or tinted moisturizer, here are some simple steps to choose just the right color:

1. Makeup artist Maria Maio recommends you go to a department store and have a consultant at a makeup counter apply a color that matches your preteen or teen's skin tone. She should wear the color all day to see if she likes it.
2. Do the same at other counters on different days.
3. Buy the foundation or tinted moisturizer you liked best. If it's too expensive, dab a sample on a piece of white paper and take that with you to a drugstore or supermarket. Another company probably makes the same color for a lot less.

For olive and darker skin tones, custom blending at a makeup counter is preferable. You can buy the department store brand or dab it on a piece of white paper and then go choose from a line of products at your favorite drugstore. The major brands all make wonderful colors for women of all skin tones. Be careful with products catering to Caucasian women because they could make olive and darker skin look ashy, pink, or yellow.

CONCEALER

Concealer should be one shade lighter than the foundation or tinted moisturizer color. If it looks orange, it is likely in the wrong color family. Be careful it is not too light because that can make your daughter look as if she has raccoon eyes. Concealers come in creams, liquids, and sticks. They are great to use in covering up pimples, blemishes, and circles under the eyes. For covering up pimples and acne, Maria Maio recommends using a dry concealer stick. Neutrogena Skin Clearing Blemish Concealer contains salicylic acid, which actually dries up the pimple while masking the blemish. It is a great product that will help your tween get over the pimple hump as she grows up. For concealing under-eye circles, Maria prefers a more emollient concealer because skin around the eyes tends to be dryer. Cover Girl Invisible Concealer is a really nice product to cover under-eye circles, scratches, and blemishes. It is applied with a wand and very easy to use.

If your daughter was born with a birthmark on her face, concealer can be a great tool to use to cover it up so she does not feel self-conscious about it. For a noticeable birthmark, try Dermablend, which is available at www.dermablend.com and at some department stores. It is really the best product to cover birthmarks on the face and the body. You could also go to a department store and have a makeup artist try different brands of concealers until you find the perfect match. But because birthmarks are so tricky to

Concealer Rules of Thumb

- For oily skin, pimples, and acne, use a dry water-based concealer stick.
- For dry skin and under-eye circles, use a creamy oil-based concealer.
- Never use a white concealer. This will make your tween look like a raccoon.

conceal I would opt for the Dermablend. It is formulated for this specific purpose. You can try a less expensive drugstore brand but you will not get the same type of coverage.

BLUSH

Blush comes in powders and creams. For young girls, a light powder applied with a blush brush is the best option. Look at your daughter's lip color to pick the blush color family that is right for her. Blush should be the shade her cheeks turn after she has been out in the cold or bronzed in the sun. Avoid cream blushes because they can look streaky if not blended properly. I also do not like the idea of a girl constantly putting her fingers in the cream; this can contaminate the makeup and make her skin break out.

EYELINER

Eyeliner is used to define eyes and make them look bigger. Eyeliner comes in pencil, powder, and liquid form. Pencils should be soft so that they go on easier. In using powder eyeliner, a thin slanted brush is dipped in eye shadow to create the line. Water can also be added to the powder to activate the color. Some liquid liners come with a wand applicator and are brushed directly onto the eyelid.

Laura Geller recommends that young girls use a pencil liner because it is the easiest to apply. Rather than a hard, scratchy one, choose a soft, creamy pencil like L'Oréal Extra-Intense Liquid Pencil Eyeliner. It is very easy to apply. For a softer look, Maria Maio recommends using a slanted brush with eye shadow to create the line.

EYE SHADOW

Eye shadow is a powder or cream formula used on the eyelids to add color and definition to the eyes. It comes in either a matte or a shimmery finish. For young girls, eye shadow with some sparkle and shine is fun and flattering. Avoid using dark colors; they can make a tween look too mature and provocative. Laura Geller suggests you buy a light pink, shimmery shadow. It looks good on everyone, and even if your tween wears too much it will just look sparkly. If you go on www.qvc.com, Laura Geller has Baked Illusion in Fresconude, which is fun, light, and shimmery. Maybelline New York also has EyeStudio, which is a shimmery palette with four different shades to play with. Laura also suggests you steer your daughter away from the heavy black and brown shadows because chances are she will use too much and look like she raided your makeup bag.

MASCARA

Mascara is a liquid product that comes with an applicator brush. It is applied to eyelashes to make them look darker, longer, and thicker. You can find waterproof mascaras, clear mascaras, and even those for sensitive eyes. Mascaras come in many different fashion colors. Maria Maio suggests choosing a mascara that matches your daughter's hair color to give her lashes a softer look. Mascara comes in many different colors, even auburn for redheads.

For cleaning the top of the mascara wand, she recommends using a plastic bag instead of a tissue to avoid tissue fibers sticking to the wand. Replace mascara every two months because it tends to get flaky and bacteria can form in the tube. Remember not to pump the mascara wand in and out of the tube because that lets air into the tube, which dries out the mascara. Inexpensive mascara is fine for a young girl. I like that you can throw it away more often and buy a new one as soon as the old tube dries up. I really like Maybelline New York Great Lash Mascara for lash volume. It is available in clear as well as black and brown so she can get the look of mascara without the drama of color. CoverGirl has a line of mascaras called Exact Eyelights, which have metallic spheres to complement your daughter's eye color. These are really fun and sparkly, especially for a party or special event. For the most perfect flake-proof, smudge-proof mascara that will never end up under the eye, Trish McEvoy High Volume or Lash Curling mascara is available at most department stores. It is a bit of a splurge, but it stays on the lashes all day, so I think it's worth it.

LIP LINER, LIPSTICK, LIP GLOSS

Note: A tween does not need lip liner or lipstick. In fact, if she uses these products she will probably look like a clown. Lip glosses are just fine, and they come in many fun colors. I would stick to that. For an older tween who wants to wear lipstick, try to find something in subtle pinks and browns. And point out to her that the problem with lip liner is that most girls choose a shade darker than their own lip color, and it looks especially ridiculous when the lipstick has worn off but the lip liner hasn't. Try to steer her toward a lip gloss with a hint of color. Be sure to buy a lip gloss that is applied directly to the lips with a wand. Those glosses that come in a pot are bacteria havens because girls stick their fingers in them all day long.

TRANSLUCENT POWDER

Translucent powder comes in a container with holes at the top as opposed to pressed powder, which comes in a compact. It is a light, smooth powder dusted over foundation with a brush. It is used to set the foundation so you have a nice dry surface when you apply powder blush and eye makeup. For even application of eye makeup, apply a thin layer of translucent powder to eyelids first. The powder creates a smooth surface and dries oily areas so the eyeliner and eye shadow will not smudge.

PRESSED POWDER

Pressed powder is heavier than translucent powder and comes in a compact. It is used to reduce shine and to seal foundation. Pressed powder can be used instead of translucent powder for a

more made-up look. Be sure to throw out the pad that comes in the compact. Dirt and oil can stick to it and be a breeding ground for bacteria. Instead, apply the pressed powder with a soft brush. To keep the brush clean, see details in the section called "Brushes" that follows.

Must-Have Makeup Tools

You could have the most beautiful makeup money can buy, but you need the right tools to apply it correctly. Here are some simple tools every girl should have at home.

MAKEUP MIRROR

A makeup mirror should have both a regular and a magnified mirror and be framed with soft, warm 10-watt frosted bulbs, not fluorescent bulbs. Always avoid florescent lights or lamps that cast a shadow on half of the face whenever you apply your makeup. I love the Jerdon Table Top Makeup Mirror available at www.amazon.com. The light is perfect for makeup application.

WEDGES

Maria Maio likes using latex sponge wedge applicators to apply foundation and concealer. They are inexpensive enough to throw out these applicators after two uses to avoid bacteria forming on the sponge.

BRUSHES

Brushes can be bought in a set or individually. Laura Geller recommends using synthetic brushes because they do not carry as much bacteria. Some must-have brushes include:

- Eyebrow comb with a brush on one side and a comb on the other
- One or two soft blush brushes for blush and translucent powder
- Eye shadow brush with a soft rounded tip
- A square-shaped cake eyeliner brush for liquid liner and for making precise lines with powder

Tips for Cleaning Your Brushes

Brushes should be cleaned weekly and especially after your daughter has had a cold. Maria Maio recommends washing the bristles with baby shampoo and water. Let them air dry overnight.

Complete Makeup

A young girl rarely needs a complete makeup application unless it is a special occasion. But it is good to know how to do it and then scale it back for everyday circumstances. The makeup that I describe in the following list is appropriate for day or evening. However, I strongly recommend using more subtle shadows and colors for daytime. It takes about ten minutes to apply these products, depending on the precision desired. Always have her start with a clean face and put on a light moisturizer. If your daughter is doing it herself, have her turn on the makeup mirror lights and begin the makeup application with item one on this list. If you are applying it, have her sit by the window so you can see her in natural light. If it is evening, make sure you have good light so you can see the colors you are applying.

To help you understand these basic makeup application tips, look at the instructional videos on www.maybelline.com. They are easy to follow for both you and your daughter:

1. Concealer: With a finger or makeup wedge, dab some concealer on anything she wants to hide, such as blemishes and pimples. For dark circles under the eyes, dab concealer there both before and after applying foundation.

2. Foundation or tinted moisturizer: Using a wedge or two fingers, pat foundation or tinted moisturizer on the right cheek, the left cheek, forehead, chin, and nose. Blend the foundation with light downward strokes to make sure that facial hairs are all lying downward, in the same direction, rather than sticking up. Blend the foundation down from the chin

onto the neck so there is no makeup line. Lift up the mirror to look at skin at different angles to ensure that the foundation is spread evenly.

3. Powder: With a big brush, dust a translucent powder (one shade lighter than your foundation) over face and eyelids to seal the foundation. Apply extra powder to eyelids to provide a clean slate for color. Powder seals liquid, so no extra foundation or concealer should be applied after this point.

4. Eyeliner: There are different types of eyeliner and each requires a different technique for application.

   • For shadow liner: Dip an angled brush into the color. Holding the brush like a pencil, draw close to the lash line from the inner to the outer corner, making a thicker line with the brush as you move outward.

   • For pencil liner: Apply liner under the bottom lashes using a dull-pointed pencil. Do not use pencil inside the lid. For the upper lid, draw a line as close to the lash line as possible. With a cotton swab, smudge the liner for a softer look.

   • For liquid liner: Apply as you would a pencil liner, but do not use on the bottom lid because it can get really messy. In general, I would not recommend liquid liner. It is hard to apply and can look really harsh if not applied properly.

5. Eye shadow: To apply eye shadow, dip a round-tip eye shadow brush into a pot of color. Blow the excess color off the brush. Apply color to the lid. Apply darker tones close to the lash line and in the crease. Tones should get lighter as you go up the lid. Use variations of one color like pink. Multicolored eyelids tend to look cheap and overdone.

6. Mascara: Apply one coat of mascara in upward sweeps holding the brush horizontally. For lashes that look full and firm, let the first coat dry before applying a second coat. For close-set eyes, use mascara only on the outer corner lashes. For wide-set eyes, use more mascara on the lashes close to the nose.

7. Blush: With a blush brush, apply powder blush or bronzer to upper cheeks on the bone and to temples. Dust nose and chin as well.

8. Lip gloss: Apply a coat of lip gloss.

Everyday Three-Minute Makeup

When she does not have much time to put on her makeup, your daughter's goal should be to enhance and define rather than to add color. This is really the only type of makeup she should need at a young age. For older tweens, eyeliner or mascara, blush, some concealer for blemishes, and lip gloss are fine. For younger tweens, stay away from the eye makeup; it will make her look too mature. If she is desperate for it, clear mascara is a good compromise.

1. Dab some concealer under the eyes and on blemishes.

2. Apply pencil eyeliner at the outer corners of the top lid and then under the lower lashes.

3. Apply a coat of mascara.

4. Brush on a little blush to give cheeks a glow.

5. Put on some lip gloss. Lip gloss is quick and easy and she does not need to be precise. It also comes in a host of different

colors so any tween can feel like she is getting color without the full coverage of a lipstick.

Eyebrows

Nicely shaped eyebrows are essential in makeup application. Even though your tween may apply her makeup perfectly, if her eyebrows grow together or look like two lightning bolts, it ruins the look. If your daughter has just a few hairs growing in the area above her nose, between her two brows, you can tweeze or shave it yourself.

However, if her eyebrows and the hair between them are thick she needs a shaping. Maria Maio does not recommend waxing because it is not precise enough. Instead, she recommends you take her to a threading salon where they remove hair quickly with a thread. (See the discussion of threading in chapter 5, "Bonding over Getting Rid of Unwanted Hair.") They do eyebrows cheaply and they do them *every day*. They are experts. Have them create the right shape for your daughter. Then you can maintain the shape at home.

If you decide to do it yourself, here are some techniques to create beautiful, symmetrical eyebrows. All you will need is a set of sharp, pointed, angled tweezers. Before shaping your daughter's brows, go to www.tweezerman.com. This company makes my favorite brow tools, and they have an easy-to-follow instructional video on the website.

DEFINING EYEBROWS

1. Place a pencil vertically along the side of your daughter's nose to the inside corner of her right eye. Mark the point where the pencil hits the brow bone with a dab of eye shadow or an eye pencil. Repeat with the left eye. With a quick upward motion, move any hairs growing between the two marks. Always tweeze in the direction the hair grows.

2. Place a pencil at an angle from the bottom right edge of her nose to the outer corner of her right eye. Mark where the pencil hits the brow bone. Remove hairs to the right of the mark. Repeat on the left eye.

3. Have her look straight ahead, hold a pencil vertically so that it crosses over her pupil. Mark where the pencil crosses the brow bone. This is where the peak of the arch should fall. Tweeze hairs above, below, and to either side of this line to emphasize the arch at this point.

4. Comb eyebrow hairs down. Cut hairs hanging beneath the brow line to the shape of the brow.

5. If brows do not follow a smooth line, pencil in the ideal shape with a strong outline. Always make an arc, never a straight vertical line. Tweeze hairs outside of this line.

CHANGING THE SHAPE OF YOUR DAUGHTER'S BROWS

If your tween's brows are too arched, use a pencil to make them more linear:

1. Remove hairs only from the top and inside corner of the brow if necessary.
2. Fill in the area just under the arch with an eye pencil using tiny strokes.

If brows are too straight, first form the peak of the arch, and then create the two ends of the arch:

1. Tweeze underneath the center of the brow to form a natural arch, curving the brow line toward the nose.
2. At the inside corner of the brow, fill in the triangle with a pencil.
3. Extend the brow in a slightly downward sweep at the outer corner.

If your daughter's brows are too thick, you must thin them before you shape them:

1. Tweeze random hairs within the arch to thin it out. All hairs below and above the arch should be removed.
2. Use a dark pencil to draw the ideal shape and thickness of her brow.
3. Tweeze the hairs outside the ideal shape.

For eyes set far apart from one another, shape brows by beginning them near the nose and ending them just inside the outer edges of the eyes.

If eyes are set close together, begin brows beyond the inner corners and arch them outside of the irises (the colored part) and end them outside the outer corners of the eyes.

* * *

Almost every girl loves makeup. It is hard as a parent to see your little girl put makeup on when she clearly is beautiful without it. However, makeup for girls is a right of passage. It makes them feel more grown up and in control of their appearance. If you approach the subject of wearing makeup with her open-mindedly and with a sense of play, it can be a way of coming together instead of constantly being pushed apart.

The best way I have found to do this is to be my daughter's guinea pig. Go to a cosmetics counter and have her tell you what she likes for you. Be a good sport even if you do not like it. Be her doll for the day. Go home and have her practice applying makeup on you. Then, she may be more likely to let you do the same for her. Use the simple techniques illustrated in this chapter to use makeup to enhance her natural beauty rather than make her look older and more mature. Experiment with different colors and enjoy your mommy-daughter time. If you forbid makeup, you run the risk of alienating her, and she will probably overdo it when you finally allow her to wear makeup. Instead, find the compromise and have fun with it together.

Bonding Activities

- Go to a makeup counter in a department store and have them do your makeup and your daughter's. (Be sure everything is disposable and sanitized before you let them put anything on her face.)

- Make a work chart for her to earn lip gloss or makeup money. If she reads half an hour each night, she gets a lip gloss at the end of the week. This totally got my daughter to read.
- Let her do your makeup. I know you may come out looking like a clown, but she will LOVE it!
- Go to a salon that specializes in eyebrows and each of you have your eyebrows shaped.
- Go to the drugstore and buy lots of inexpensive makeup in different colors so she can experiment and play.
- Make your own lip gloss. Go to www.creativekidsathome. com for great recipes.
- Go to www.creativityforkids.com and get the Make Your Own Lip Balm kit. This is such a fun activity to do with your daughter and her friends.
- At www.FashionAngelsEnterprises.com you can order their Make-Up Artist Sketch Portfolio. She can use the stencils to sketch her favorite make-up looks. My daughter takes her portfolio with her everywhere she goes. It is fun and creative!

CHAPTER 4

Bonding over Her Hands & Feet

This chapter embodies the essence of my message to moms. Your daughter wants to spend time with you *and* to feel you think of her as a young woman, not as a baby. Giving her salon-type manicures and pedicures at home is an easy way to engage her and make her feel pretty at the same time. She will love the pampering, and you will love that her hands and feet look clean and neat.

Let's face it: hands and feet speak volumes about a person. When you meet a person and she shakes your hand with sharp, raggedy-edged, or dirty fingernails, you immediately want to pull your hand away. When people are chewing their nails, they look nervous or seem to lack confidence. If a woman's nail polish is chipped, she appears as if she could use a lesson in basic grooming. It's gross when flip-flops or summer sandals display dirty, uncut toenails. Helping your daughter learn how to keep her hands and feet healthy and groomed is an invaluable lesson she will take through life. It also means her admirers will focus on the beauty of her personality rather than be distracted by a lack of attention to personal hygiene.

Unfortunately, hands and feet aren't simply about manicures and pedicures. In this chapter you will find ways to treat nail biting, athlete's foot, warts, foot odor, and other common hand and foot problems. Even if your tween does not have foot issues now, you'll learn about ways to prevent future problems through proper preventative care. So, read on and you will find the path to great hands and feet.

Need to Know

Base coat—A coat of clear polish applied before the nail color. Some brands offer base coats that contain nail strengtheners such as protein, aloe vera, vitamin E, and calcium.

Buffer—Buffing tools come in various shapes and grades: discs, blocks, and sticks (like emery boards); depending on the grade, they can be used to smooth rough nail edges or to buff the surface of nails to create a smoother, shinier surface.

Cuticle cream—Cream or lotion that softens and moisturizes rough, dry cuticles.

Cuticle nippers—Special scissors used to cut loose, dry cuticles. (Note: I do not like to use these on young girls because cutting their cuticles is really unnecessary.)

Nail brightener—A product that claims to make nail beds look pinker and tips appear whiter so nails look healthy even without nail polish.

Nail clippers or scissors—Used to trim nails and toenails; scissors are often preferable for better precision on small fingers and toes.

Nail file (sometimes called an emery board)—Used to smooth out nail edges and to shape nails.

Nail strengthener—Serum that may include proteins, natural oils, gelatin, and even nylon fibers; usually looks like clear polish and is applied as a base coat or alone to strengthen weak nails.

Orange stick—A wooden stick used to remove dirt or excess polish.

Pumice stone—Used during a pedicure to smooth rough patches of dry skin.

Top coat—A coat of clear polish applied after the nail color to make the color last longer.

Hand and Foot Care 101

While there is no consensus on when a girl should be allowed to wear nail polish, all mothers will agree there is nothing worse than long, broken, dirty nails. I think it is really important for kids to be kids. They should play and get dirty without worry. And if a girl is working on a piece of clay sculpture in art class at school, she should really get into her project rather than worry about chipping her nail polish or breaking a nail. To that end, it is best to keep your daughter's nails reasonably short. Short nails are neat nails. They should just touch the end of the fingertip. A light clear coat of polish or nail brightener keeps nails looking fresh and healthy.

If your daughter wants to wear a color and you are up for it, try an at-home mani-pedi or take her to a salon with you for a mother-daughter beauty afternoon. If you opt for the salon treatment, bring your own tools. While salons claim to sterilize their equipment, it is still easy to catch nail fungus or warts from tools that were not cleaned properly. Those machines with the blue light do little to properly sterilize the tools.

At-Home Manicures and Pedicures

Giving your daughter a manicure and a pedicure could not be easier. You just need a few simple things from your local drugstore and a little bit of time in which to play. You can even choose to do her nails the same day each week so you get into the habit of weekly grooming. It is a nice treat and something you can do together.

MANICURE

If you want your tween to do her homework, but she can't concentrate—or doesn't want to—you may try giving her an incentive. Promise her that when she finishes her homework, you'll give her a manicure. Or if she needs a study break, offer to give her a manicure as long as she promises to finish her homework when her nails dry.

Here are the simple steps for an easy at-home manicure:

1. Find a hard surface: I like the kitchen table because you can sit across from her. If you are going to use polish or polish remover, cover the surface with a towel and make sure there is good ventilation because these products tend to have a harsh smell.
2. Remove polish: Clean off old polish with cotton and nail polish remover.
3. File: Use a large sturdy file, and file both ways using tiny strokes. If you file in only one direction, you may shape the nail into a point.
4. Smooth cuticles: Apply cuticle cream to the cuticles and gently push cuticles back with an orange stick wrapped in cotton or a cotton swab. OPI Avoplex Cuticle treatment or cuticle oil can be found in the drugstore and is one of my favorites to care for the cuticles.
5. Buff: Use a very fine-grain nail buffer to buff off ridges and nicks on the nails.
6. Clean: Remove dirt from beneath the nails with a cotton swab or orange stick dipped in nail polish remover.
7. Polish: If you do not want to polish her nails, you can try a

nail brightener, such as Nicole by OPI Nic's Sticks, using the technique below to keep them looking healthy.

a. Start with the same fingernail when applying multiple coats so each coat has a little time to set.

b. Apply a base coat with even strokes to each nail. It is important to apply a clear base coat to prevent nails from being discolored by nail polish.

c. Apply one coat of polish to each nail, and then apply a second coat.

d. Apply a clear top coat after the final coat of color has dried for two minutes.

8. Dry: Keep hands still for at least fifteen minutes to allow all of the polish to dry thoroughly.

Tip: A nice light-pink polish is always pretty and clean looking. Chipping is more noticeable on darker polishes. For a little extra sparkle, try the color "Love Your Life" from Nicole by OPI. The bottle is filled with hearts and sparkles. It is a great compromise if you do not want her to wear a color because it is just clear polish with sparkles added to it.

PEDICURE

There is nothing I love more than treating my daughter's sweet little feet and making her feel like a princess. At home, my daughter sits on one of her little chairs at her play table, and I put a towel on the floor and place a bucket of warm water on the towel. My daughter soaks her feet in the bucket, and I use a scrub and any other fun things I can find to massage and clean her feet.

Then I moisturize her feet and legs, trim her nails, and polish her toes. Creativity for Kids makes Pretty Pedicure Salon, with all the items you will need for a great pedicure. It's available at www. creativityforkids.com.

To make a pedicure at home feel truly luxurious, find a comfortable chair for her to sit in. At her feet, place a bucket of warm water on a towel. (I use the baby bathtub I got from the hospital when I brought her home as an infant!) Buy an inexpensive scrub or make your own. The scrub will exfoliate her feet and lower legs and make her feel fabulous! Any light moisturizer for the massage will do. The key is to do as many luxurious things as possible so she feels like she is getting the full treatment.

1. Trim: Cut her nails straight across with a large, straight-edged toenail clipper.
2. File: File the rough edges of the nail with a fine emery board. Square-shaped nails are best to avoid ingrown toenails.
3. Soak: Soak her feet for five to ten minutes in warm water. You can add some bubble bath and Epsom salts to the water to make it a little fancier.
4. Exfoliate: Put a dime-size amount of body scrub in your hand. Rub the rough skin on her heels and toes. She will love this! Try using one of the sugar scrubs described in chapter 2, "Bonding over How She Cares for Her Skin." Rinse off the scrub with the water from the bucket.
5. Clean: Brush her nails and feet with a wet nail brush and soap. Then, stick her feet back in the bucket to rinse. Dry her feet well.

6. Moisturize: Massage her feet with cream and give her a nice foot massage. (See the foot massage description that follows.)

7. Separate her toes: Take a long strip of toilet paper and twist it so it looks like a snake. Wrap her toes as follows: Put the snake between her big toe and the second toe. Then pull it up through the space between the second and third toes. Go back down through the space between the third and fourth toes. Pull it back up between the fourth and the pinkie toes.

8. Polish: Apply polish to her toenails as you would to her fingernails (see the previous section). Let the polish dry. Don't let your daughter wear anything other than flip-flops for at least half an hour.

How to Give a Foot Massage

1. Apply a moisturizer that moves easily. (There are various creams just for the feet, which come in peppermint and aloe, but you can use any moisturizer you have at home. Baby oil is great too.) Rub the cream all over one foot at a time.

3. Alternating hands, gently press your thumb knuckles into the tendon on the bottom of the foot. The tendon is the tender area between the pad and the heel.

4. Next, massage the toes. Lift the pinkie toe with the forefinger and thumb. Gently rotate the toe. Do the same for each toe.

5. Press the area around either side of the ankle gently.

6. Cup the heel of the foot with both hands and rub back and forth.

Troubleshooting and Treating Common Nail and Foot Problems

With the stress of school and social life, combined with communal showers, pools, and kids walking around barefoot anywhere they can, it is no wonder our girls come home with all sorts of nasty hand and foot problems. Fortunately, there are many ways to make fingernails and toenails healthier and prettier, and there is an easy solution to more serious problems right in your drugstore.

WEAK, YELLOW, OR DRY NAILS

Nails that split and peel, are dry and flaky, or have a yellow tinge are not very attractive. There are essential nutrients you can increase in your daughter's diet (or your own, should you be experiencing any of these problems) to help improve the health of her nails (see "Bonding over Nutrition & Fitness," chapter 7). But there are also simple steps you can take to improve the appearance of her nails.

If her nails split or peel, cut her nails so they are all even. Massage a nail conditioning cream into her nails and cuticles. Apply a nail strengthener. You can use the nail strengthener alone or you can apply polish over it. When using nail strengthener alone, apply a coat every other day.

If her nails are yellowed because of the use of nail polish, try using a nail brightener either alone or under nail polish. You can purchase nail brighteners, but an inexpensive at-home option is lemon juice. Simply dip the nails in lemon juice for five to ten minutes. (Do not attempt this if she has any cuts or open wounds on her hands because it will sting.) If the nails are stained from some other substance, the lemon juice may work alone, or you can try buffing the stains out. You can also try soaking the nails in a mixture of hydrogen peroxide and water. Be aware these techniques can dry the nails and skin. Be sure to moisturize afterward.

For dry fingernails, moisturize her hands and nails each day with a cream designed specifically for hands and nails.

For dry, jagged, or overgrown cuticles, exfoliate and use a cuticle cream daily. Warn your daughter not to bite or rip them! They can start bleeding and become really painful or even infected.

NAIL BITING

Is your daughter a nail biter? It is such a bad habit, yet many girls do it. It is important for you to make sure she understands what happens when she bites her nails. First of all, germs from surfaces she touched get in her mouth and can make her sick. Second, the saliva from her mouth, combined with the chewing, weakens her nails. Last, biting her nails makes her look insecure. So, how do you get her to quit? Here are a few suggestions:

- Reward her with a manicure if she stops.
- Use a bad-tasting product designed for nail biters on nails and cuticles every day for a month. The taste is so awful it should condition her to stop.
- Have her wear gloves when she's around the house so she has nothing to bite.
- Keep her nails neatly polished so she can appreciate how

nice it is to have pretty nails and so she has an incentive to keep them nice.

- Give her something else to chew, like carrot sticks.

ATHLETE'S FOOT

It's easy to pick up the athlete's foot ringworm in communal showers, locker rooms, and swimming pools. The symptoms are burning and itching between the toes and, often, broken skin. Athlete's foot is also caused by rises in temperature, wet shoes, tight shoes, and socks made from synthetic fibers.

I interviewed Podiatrist Scott R. Lurie, MD, who recommended the following tips to prevent getting athlete's foot. He also offered valuable advice on the other common problems discussed in the rest of the chapter.

- Keep your feet dry and clean.
- Avoid wearing dirty socks—especially another person's dirty socks.
- Always wear flip-flops in a communal shower or by a pool.
- Use an antifungal powder in your shoes.
- Dry your feet thoroughly after a shower—especially in between each toe.
- Alternate between pairs of shoes so that the shoes you wear each day have a chance to dry out.

Treatment of Athlete's Foot

If athlete's foot occurs, treat it immediately so the infection does not spread to the toenails. Athlete's foot can be easily treated at home by following these steps twice each day:

1. Wash your feet with soap and water.
2. Dry your feet well.
3. Apply an antifungal ointment such as Tinactin. They come in creams, powders, liquid sprays, and powder aerosols.
4. Continue treatment for two weeks after symptoms go away so the infection does not return.
5. See a doctor if the condition doesn't resolve itself in two to four weeks.

FOOT ODOR

There are more bacteria in between the toes than on any other part of the body. When perspiration mixes with these bacteria, odor occurs. Wet shoes and socks make the problem even worse.

To help prevent and treat foot odor, wash feet once or twice a day with soap and water. Dry each foot well with a clean towel. (Make sure to wash and dry the area between the toes.) Cotton socks are the best material to absorb perspiration. Dr. Lurie recommends moisture-wicking socks to keep feet dry. Charcoal-insulated insoles designed to control odor should be put into all shoes. Again, it is also a good idea to have her alternate shoes instead of wearing the same pair every day. For more odor controlling tips, see chapter 6, "Bonding over Puberty & Hygiene."

CALLUSES AND CORNS

Calluses and corns are caused by pressure on the feet. Tight and ill-fitting shoes and activities such as dance class, athletics, and walking around the mall with friends for hours can leave a girl with corns. The skin's natural defense against this pressure is to create an extra layer, which appears as a callus on the ball of the foot or a corn on the bony part of the toe. Calluses are larger, rougher, and have no central core. They are usually found on the sole or heel. Corns are smooth circular bumps with a core of hard or soft tissue. They are found on the tops or sides of toes.

Although medicine may help to remove the callus or corn, it does not address the problem: pressure.

Treatment

Here's what Dr. Lurie recommends for treating calluses and corns:

1. Soak feet for five minutes in warm water. Dry feet well.
2. Do not use over-the-counter treatments with salicylic acid because they can burn the skin. Also avoid all cutting instruments.
3. Put a nonmedicated callus/corn pad on the affected area. The pad alleviates some of the pressure. Have your daughter wear the pads daily until the callus/corn starts to disappear.
4. File the corn gently with a corn file or pumice stone.
5. To prevent the callus/corn from coming back, she needs to wear better fitting shoes.

Have her continue to use the pads to alleviate any pressure from other shoes. While treating calluses, use an insole or air cushion in her shoes.

WARTS

Kids are the most common sufferers from warts. A wart is a rough-textured growth (usually small and round) on the skin. They often appear on hands and feet. Because warts are caused by a viral infection in the top layer of the skin, they require medication.

Prevention and Treatment of Warts

To prevent warts, always treat cuts on the hands and feet to prevent the virus from getting under the skin.

Stress also contributes to the spread of the virus because stress suppresses the immune system, letting the virus grow unchecked. (Check out some stress-relieving treatments in chapter 8, "Bonding over Aromatherapy to Feel Beautiful.")

Treatment

Share these simple steps from Dr. Lurie with your daughter.

Some warts may be treated at home; others may have to be removed surgically. To remove a wart at home, try the following:

1. Soak hands/feet in warm water for five to ten minutes.
2. With an emery board or pumice, scrape the skin surrounding the wart. Do not cut it.
3. Apply an over-the-counter wart medication to the problem area only.

If the wart is painful or there is a cluster of warts, you should see a doctor for treatment. Be aware that the doctor treats warts with much stronger salycilic acid (60 percent) than you can buy in the store (15 percent), so you can probably get rid of the wart faster and prevent it from spreading if you take your daughter to see a doctor right away. The doctor can also remove a wart surgically or with lasers.

INGROWN TOENAILS

Ingrown toenails are often caused by fan-shaped nails, which are nails that curve in at the side. Fan-shaped nails pinch the skin, often breaking it, which allows bacteria to get in. Ingrown nails are also caused by shoes that pinch the toe, forcing the nail to grow into the flesh.

Treatment

Make sure you do not cut too much off the edges of her toenails when trimming them. Square, straight toenails are the best.

If your daughter is having toe pain, she should see a podiatrist. To relieve the discomfort at home, Dr. Scott Lurie recommends these basic steps:

1. Soak both feet in a bath of warm water and Epsom salts and wash the area with soap.
2. Dry the feet and toes thoroughly.
3. Put a small piece of cotton between the nail and the flesh and secure with some surgical tape or a bandage. Leave the cotton there for a day.
4. Apply a topical antibiotic ointment.
5. If the pain does not go away, see a doctor.

NAIL FUNGUS

Nail fungus is caused by fungal organisms that invade the nail and nail root. It is transmitted in moist public environments like pool decks and locker rooms.

Treatment

Topical over-the-counter medications are by and large ineffective. Prescription medication is often needed.

Dr. Lurie cautions against allowing nail salons to use their own instruments on you or your daughter. Most places do not sterilize their equipment adequately. Ten seconds under the blue light and five minutes in the pink solution do not make them sterile. Bring your own instruments if you decide to go to a nail salon. Clean them properly at home before and after your visit to the salon. Leaving the instruments in alcohol overnight is the best way to clean them. But remember, even then they will not be surgically sterile.

✳ ✳ ✳

I hope you enjoy pampering your girl as much as I do. If your daughter resists nail trimming, the at-home mani-pedi could be just the thing to get her nails in shape. My friend's mom once told me the first thing people notice when they meet you are your hands, your hair, and your teeth. If they look good, people focus on other things. But if they look bad, all they will remember are your dirty fingernails, messy hair, and yellow teeth. Teaching your daughter to take pride in her hands and feet the way she does in the rest of her appearance is an important life lesson.

Spending this kind of time together can also be a bonding experience. I have a friend who was going through a divorce and her ten-year-old daughter had a lot of anger. Her daughter would not talk about her feelings, and my friend was so busy with work and getting dinner on the table, she did not know how to get her daughter talking. I suggested she stop for ten minutes on a Saturday and give her daughter a pedicure. My friend discovered it was a way to get her daughter to relax and start to talk. She did not talk about her feelings right away, but it began a dialogue with mom.

Although giving your daughter a pedicure is not the answer to all of life's problems, the time spent just focusing on her can give you an opportunity to chat and forge a closer relationship.

Bonding Activities

- Give your daughter an at-home manicure or pedicure.
- Treat her to a hand or foot massage before bed.
- Go to the salon together and let the manicurist put some polish on her nails.
- Invite some of her friends over for a mani-pedi party.
- Make a study chart through which your daughter can earn Pretty Pedicure Salon or Ultimate Nail Studio by Creativity for Kids.

CHAPTER 5

Bonding over Getting Rid of Unwanted Hair

No matter how old you are, getting rid of unwanted hair is a daunting task. In fact, for many women it is the bane of their existence. If you are the mother of a young girl whose body is changing, it can be an even greater challenge. Girls get hair between their eyebrows, above their lip, under their arms, and even on their forearms all before puberty. But what should you do about it and when is the right time to take action?

It is always important to consider how you would feel if you were in your daughter's shoes before you tell her she is too young to worry about these things. Kids in school can be mean. It can take years to build up a girl's self-esteem and just a little teasing to destroy it. So, when it comes to any type of facial hair, you should consider removing it if it bothers her. If you are hesitant to take action, consider how cruel kids can be. They may snicker that she has a mustache or call her a werewolf if her brows grow together. No mother wants that. Sometimes, the hair may not be dark but she still may be self-conscious about it.

In this chapter, you will see how simple it can be to help your daughter through this sensitive time so she feels her best and can concentrate on more important things. After all, as women, we know that when we're uncomfortable with how we look, it's hard to feel great about ourselves. Nevertheless, many mothers are sensitive about the subject of how old their daughters should be before they can remove unwanted hair. If you're reluctant, let me say that I believe my job as a mom is to build my daughter's self-esteem and help her feel confident, and this is one area where it's important to be compassionate.

Dark hair on the face and body can occur during the tween years. Once it's there, whether it's on the face or at the bikini line, you need to remove it. Please don't get me wrong: I am *not* promoting a Brazilian wax for twelve-year-olds. However, allowing your daughter to have hair sticking out from under her bathing suit is as bad as letting her walk around with dirt under her fingernails or snot dripping from her nose. It's just not pretty.

This chapter is going to tell you everything you need to know about shaving, waxing, tweezing, threading, depilatories, lasers, and electrolysis. I am going to tell you what to do where and when to do it. Most importantly, I am going to dispel myths you may have heard. As you know, I want your daughter to look to you as a source of comfort and unconditional love. Before you give her a knee-jerk reaction to her desire to shave her legs, read this chapter and see whether insisting that she wait until she is twelve was your mother's idea or is what you truly believe.

The Big Hair Removal Questions

Let's start by dispelling some of the most common myths about hair growth and removal.

Dear Erika: My prepubescent daughter has a mustache, and her brows grow together. She will not tolerate the pain of waxing. What can I do?

You should absolutely SHAVE the hair or use a depilatory, an agent for removing hair.

Many women believe that shaving causes hair to come back coarser and darker, like a man's beard. That is a MYTH. You won't have to shave or use a depilatory very often (probably no more than every other week). Shaving is painless and safe for all skin types. Depilatories are good as long as your tween's skin is not overly sensitive.

Dear Erika: My nine-year-old daughter wants to shave her legs and underarms, but I think she is too young. What do I do?

Ask yourself the following questions:

- Does your daughter have visible hair in these areas?
- What color is the hair?
- Can you see the body hair from two feet away?
- Is she asking only because she has some friends who are starting to shave, or are most of her friends already shaving?
- Are you comfortable with her handling a razor?

Young girls look forward to the rites of womanhood. Doing certain things makes them feel grown up, something you may not be comfortable with. But your daughter may also have some real, legitimate concerns about the hair on her body. If she has a fair amount of visible, darker hair on her body, why shouldn't she shave? You may have to ask yourself what issues you have with your daughter growing up. Would you want to go to school with hairy legs where the slightest imperfection can bring on teasing and poor self-esteem? If she wants to shave, what's the big deal?

If you do not allow her to shave, she might borrow a friend's razor and cut up her legs. I think it's best to show your daughter empathy and be grateful she feels comfortable enough to talk openly about a subject that may be highly sensitive to her. Being intolerant or judgmental will just alienate her and make her feel you don't understand.

Dear Erika: Swimsuit season is approaching. Her bikini line is less than perfect, and she is only eleven. What do I do?

You should not tell her she is too young to get a bikini wax and let her walk around with pubic hair hanging out of her bathing suit. If she can tolerate the pain of waxing, it is a great option. Otherwise, let her shave or help her use a depilatory. Just remove the hair that would stick out from under a bathing suit. Do not forget to look at your daughter from behind; hair grows in the buttocks area, too, and there will be plenty of times when she sits down in her bathing suit that hair in this area, if not removed, would be noticeable.

How to Get Rid of Hair

Many options are available for getting rid of unwanted hair. While I would like everything in this book to be a fun activity, hair removal is just a pain. However, I will give you all your options and offer you some helpful tips to make it as easy and painless as possible. Just keep reminding your daughter that every woman goes through this, including you. Tell her a funny hair removal story about yourself or one of your girlfriends just to show her you know

Need to Know

Depilatory—A cream or lotion that contains chemicals that can destroy the proteins in the hair, making the hair fall out.

Electrolysis and thermolysis—Two methods of permanent hair removal. Electrolysis uses an electrical current to destroy the hair follicle and requires a number of sessions. Thermolysis follows a similar process but uses heat in place of the electrical current to destroy the follicle and is more efficient than electrolysis.

Ingrown hair—A hair that grows upward and then curls back down under the skin, never breaking the skin's surface. They often appear as a red bump or pimple.

Laser—A permanent hair removal method that targets the melanin in the hair follicle. The laser goes beneath the follicle to dislodge the hair.

Patch test—A trial use of a product on a small patch of skin on the arm before applying it to a large area of the body or face. Test the cream or lotion for the amount of time the product instructions suggest. This is to make sure no allergic reaction occurs and to ensure that the product works the way it claims it will (in terms of time and effectiveness).

Shaving—A method of hair removal in which a razor is used to cut the hair at the surface of the skin.

Threading—A method of hair removal in which a cotton thread is pulled along the hair shaft in a quick twisting motion. The hair is trapped in a tiny loop and is lifted from the follicle.

Strip waxing—A method of hair removal in which hot wax is applied to an area, a strip of linen is pressed into the wax, the strip is quickly ripped off the skin, and the hair under the wax is pulled off with it.

Stripless waxing—A method of hair removal used on more sensitive areas in which hot wax is applied to an area and then ripped off by hand, taking the hair under the wax with it. Generally, stripless wax is a lower temperature and adheres only to hair, not the skin, so it is less painful.

what she's feeling. Also be sure to help her realize the issue of body hair is nothing to worry or feel bad about. It's just a part of life.

SHAVING

Typically, prepubescent girls are embarrassed about the sudden appearance of hair and they want to get rid of it painlessly. Shaving is great for girls at this age. I encourage you to teach your daughter how to shave as a first step. If you are uncomfortable with her handling a razor, you can do it for her. In fact, you should always be the only one to do any shaving on the face.

More permanent solutions for hair removal, such as laser or electrolysis can be considered a year after her period begins.

What Body Parts Can She Shave?

Your daughter can shave:

- Between the eyebrows
- Sideburns
- Upper lip
- Around the nipple
- Stomach
- Underarms
- Forearms
- Bikini line (this is a sensitive area, so be especially careful)
- Legs

When hair is shaved, it grows back as it originally appeared, not darker or thicker. Often women think hair is coarser because they only let it grow a quarter of an inch. If a girl lets it grow out to an inch, she will see the hair is the same as before she shaved it. Try it once and you will see. How often your daughter needs to shave depends on her genetics. The bottom line about frequency of shaving is simple: when hair is visible, she will have to shave the area again.

Tools for Shaving

For the best shave, your daughter will need the following:

- Razor: Use a razor with changeable blades, a pivoting head, and a handle that is easy to grip, even with soapy hands. I don't like disposable razors because the handle is hard to grip, and they rarely have pivoting heads, which makes hard-to-reach areas inaccessible. I like the Venus razor best.
- Razor blade: Use only the razor blade specifically designed to fit the razor she uses. Do not mix brands because if the blade does not fit the razor, the risk of cutting or nicking increases. Always have her use a high-quality twin blade with an aloe strip.
- Shaving cream: A nice thick shaving cream or gel will give a better shave than soap does. It will also form a track as she shaves so she doesn't miss a spot.
- Shower gel: This is optional, but I like to mix a little shower gel with shaving cream to leave my legs even smoother.

How to Shave

1. Apply a thick layer of shaving cream to the area. (Mix the shaving cream with shower gel in the palm of your hand before application for a smoother shave.)

2. With one hand, gently stretch the skin you are about to shave. Then, pressing lightly, shave in the direction that feels most comfortable.

3. Shave in one steady stroke, then rinse the blade. Repeat the stroke-and-rinse process until you've shaved the entire area. Never wipe the blade with a towel or tissue. This dulls the blade.

4. After shaving, dry the skin with a towel and apply an alcohol-free moisturizer or baby oil to lock in moisture without irritating the skin.

Shaving Tips

- Shaving should be the last thing she does in the shower. The steam opens up the pores, which allows for a closer shave.
- She should rinse the blade with warm water between strokes.
- Change the blade every five to seven uses or when it seems dull.
- Never dry shave! It can cause irritation and red bumps, and even lead to ingrown hairs.
- If shaving causes her to develop ingrown hairs, try exfoliating the skin before shaving.
- If skin gets irritated and has itchy red bumps the day after she shaves, try the following:
  - Change the razor blade because the bumps could be due to abrasion.

- Have her stop using her shaving cream because she may be allergic to it.
- Avoid applying moisturizer directly after shaving.
- Tell her not to shave right before she goes to the beach. The salt water and sunscreen can irritate her legs.
- Order Bikini Bump Blaster by Completely Bare online at www.completelybare.com. It's really a great product for reducing those red bumps.

WAXING

Waxing is an effective yet painful method of hair removal. Many girls like waxing because hair does not grow back for four to six weeks. However, hair has to be at least one-quarter of an inch long in order to be waxed, so it requires her to be hairy for a while before she can wax again.

Waxing can be done in a salon or at home. Before waxing your daughter's legs or teaching her how to do it, go to a professional at least once to see how it is done. Once you learn how to do it, you can wax your daughter at home. Cindy Barshop, owner of Completely Bare salons in New York City, recommends taking your daughter to a reputable salon that specializes in hair removal rather than to a nail salon that also offers waxing services. The hair removal salon should offer both strip and stripless waxing for sensitive areas. If you decide to go to a salon on a regular basis rather than trying waxing at home, here are some tips for best results:

- Be a good client by becoming a steady client. Have the same person wax your daughter each time she visits the salon. She will get better treatment and better results because the beautician will get used to her skin and the thickness of her hair. She may also take more time with your daughter, tweezing out every last hair.
- Watch for cleanliness. The beautician should always:
  - Use a fresh wooden stick every time she dips into the wax.
  - Use sterilized tweezers to remove in-grown hairs (or bring your own).
  - Apply an aloe lotion after the area has been waxed.

If you feel confident in your ability to wax, you can jump right into waxing at home. Doing so is considerably less expensive than at a salon, especially if you want to wax several areas of the body. You can buy wax and cloth strips in a beauty supply store or pharmacy. Completely Bare has a terrific waxing kit that can be bought on their website (www.completelybare.com). I like this kit because it is the exact same wax they use in the salons. Their website also has step-by-step instructions and illustrations for at-home waxing. You can try to find a good wax in your local pharmacy, but I have found that many just do not work well.

Be forewarned: waxing is messy. The wax will most likely drip onto the floor or onto whatever she is sitting on. But if you place your pot of wax on a flat surface that is covered with tin foil, and you cover your furniture with newspaper or something to absorb any drops of wax that may fall, you should have no problem.

If your daughter is going away to camp, waxing is a great

option. It should get her through at least four weeks without having to bother with a razor.

What Body Parts Can She Wax?

Your daughter can wax:

- Eyebrows—salon only
- Sideburns—salon only
- Upper lip—at home or in a salon (A salon is best because you could burn her face if the wax is too hot.)
- Underarms—at home or in a salon
- Forearms—at home or in a salon
- Stomach—at home or in a salon
- Bikini line—at home or in a salon, but I recommend a salon
- Legs—at home or in a salon

Tools for Waxing

For the best waxing, you will need:

- Linen or other cloth strips: These are used to remove the wax and hair.
- Wooden sticks: Tongue depressors like the ones the doctor puts in your mouth during a check-up are excellent for applying wax to the skin and spreading it evenly.
- Strip and/or stripless wax: The best waxes are soft and come off easily. Avoid waxes that are difficult to remove with the linen or other cloth strips. Experiment with different waxes. In my research I have not found cold wax strips and cold wax kits to be as efficient as warm waxes. The hair may or may

not come off. If you have used them and they work for you, then you can certainly try them on your daughter. However, if her hair is thick and coarse, a warm wax kit is preferable.

- Cotton, astringent, baby powder: These articles are used in preparing and treating the skin before and after waxing.
- Aloe lotion: This moisturizes and soothes the skin after waxing.

How to Wax

Waxing lasts four to six weeks, depending on the individual's genetics. However, hair can appear just a week after waxing because it grows in cycles. The hair that appears is not the hair that was just waxed, of course, because that was removed. It is different hair in a different cycle. Wax again when visible hair is at least one-quarter of an inch long.

For ethnic hair anywhere on the face and body, it is best to try salon waxing before waxing at home. Ethnic hair tends to be coarse and requires more skill to minimize the pain.

Cindy Barshop from Completely Bare helped me put together these waxing instructions. For a detailed instructional video, see her website at www.completelybare.com.

1. With a piece of cotton saturated with an astringent, clean the area of the body you are going to wax. Wipe away the moisture and pat some baby powder on the area. With a rounded scissor, trim hair to one-quarter to one-half inch in length before waxing.

2. Warm the wax as per the instructions on the package. Stir the wax until it is an even consistency. Be sure to test the temperature of the wax on your wrist before applying it to your daughter's skin so that you do not burn her. (You can remove the test wax with a linen strip, or by hand if you are using a stripless kit.)

3. Dip the spatula in the wax and spread a thin layer of wax over a small patch of hair. Be sure to spread in the same direction the hair is growing.

4. Take a strip of the linen and press it smoothly into the wax. Let it sit for a few seconds.

5. Firmly holding down the skin just below the waxed area, pull off the linen strip in one quick motion in the opposite direction of the hair growth. Be careful to do this as close to the skin as possible, as if you are turning a page. Firmly apply pressure to the area that was just waxed to ease the pain.

6. Repeat these steps until the whole area is free of hair. Use tweezers to remove any stray hairs. Do not go over the same area more than twice.

7. Using a cotton ball, rub some astringent over the entire waxed area. Then, apply some aloe lotion to soothe the skin. After a few hours, any red bumps should disappear.

Waxing Tips

- Pull the linen off as quickly as possible in the opposite direction of the hair growth.
- Make sure the area being waxed is completely dry and free from body oils.

- Make sure hair is at least one-quarter to one-half inch long for best results. (If the hair is too short, there's little for the wax to adhere to and you won't pull much hair away.)
- Do not wax girls who are taking Accutane or using products with glycolic acid to treat acne.
- Do not wax freshly tanned skin.
- Use a wax with resin. The resin content is what makes the wax grab or not grab the hair.
- Use baby oil to remove excess wax from the skin.
- Wait a day or two before exposing any waxed area to the sun.

TWEEZING

I address tweezing eyebrows in chapter 3, "Bonding over Makeup & Brows." To put it bluntly, I do not believe little girls should walk around with a unibrow. Tweezing is also useful on other parts of the body, but it is painful, which is why I recommend shaving for younger girls. As girls get older, you can tweeze for them and teach them how to do it themselves.

What Body Parts Can She Tweeze?

Your daughter can tweeze:

- Eyebrows
- Nipple area
- Stomach
- Bikini line (Stray hairs sometimes are missed during shaving or waxing.)
- Hairs growing out of a mole (Before tweezing any hair growing out of a mole, consult with your dermatologist.)

Tools for Tweezing

For the best tweezing, your daughter will need:

- Tweezers: Use tweezers with an angled edge to properly grasp the root of the hair.
- Toner: Use toner after tweezing.

How to Tweeze

1. Tweeze only one hair at a time.
2. Grab the hair at the base with the prongs of the tweezers and give a quick, sharp pull.
3. Dab a mild toner on the tweezed area.

Go to www.Tweezerman.com for an instructional video on how to tweeze.

Tweezing Tips

1. Tweeze after a shower or hold a warm washcloth to the area to allow the pores to open and the hairs to come out more easily.
2. Clean your tweezers with alcohol to keep them clean.
3. Apply tea bags (any variety) soaked in cool water to soothe irritated skin.
4. If you tweeze correctly (pulling the hair from the root rather than just breaking the hair) the hair should not grow back for a few weeks.

THREADING

Threading is done in a salon. The technician will take a long piece of thread and, forming a tiny loop that grasps the hair, quickly remove the unwanted hair from the follicle by rolling the looped, twisted thread over the area.

I think threading is a great option for hair removal anywhere on the face. It is gentle and does not hurt as much as waxing does. If you go to a good threader, she can give eyebrows a beautiful shape with less pain than from tweezing. Threading can also be done very quickly, which is great for kids. However, it needs to be done by a professional who has lots of experience. So, I recommend going to a threading salon. They are in malls all over the country. The technicians do nothing but thread every day, so they are usually very good at it.

Try a threading salon in your area and have them shape your eyebrows first. If you like the result, and your daughter thinks she wants to give it a try, have the professional threader do her brows, sideburns, or hair above her upper lip.

DEPILATING

Using a depilatory cream or lotion is a painless method of hair removal. However, the chemicals they contain can be harsh on young, delicate skin, and some depilatory products have a strong odor that you might find objectionable. If the cream or lotion does not irritate the skin, this is a great alternative to shaving hair on the upper lip, brows, and bikini line. In my own experience, depilatory creams burned and irritated my daughter's upper lip, but they were fine to use in removing hair between her eyebrows. Although the irritation lasted only about an hour, I realized it was not the right option for her sensitive skin.

If your daughter has upper lip hair, I would do a tiny patch test first on her arm, then between the brows to see how her skin reacts. If she is okay with it, you can try the depilatory product on her upper lip. If the skin begins to burn, remove the product immediately. If it does not get irritated, I think this is a great option for hair removal on her face. If it burns, shaving, waxing, or threading is better.

What Body Parts Can She Depilate?

Your daughter can depilate:

- Between the eyebrows
- Sideburns
- Upper lip
- Stomach
- Bikini line
- Legs

Tools for Depilating

For the best depilation, your daughter will need:

- Depilatory: You can buy a depilatory cream or lotion in your local drugstore.

How to Depilate

1. Do a patch test.
2. If skin does not react negatively to the cream after eight minutes, spread a thick layer of cream on the area to cover all the hair.

3. Face—Remove the cream with a tissue and rinse the area with cold water. With a damp washcloth, rub away any hairs that did not come off on the first tissue.
4. Legs and Bikini—Remove cream in the shower with warm water.
5. Apply the soothing moisturizer included with the depilatory product to the area.

Depilating Tips

- Buy the depilatory specifically designed for the area you are working on. For example, do not use a leg depilatory on your tween's upper lip because the chemicals will be too strong for the sensitive skin on her face.

BLEACHING

Bleaching hair is an option for dark hair on the forearms and the stomach. Although many girls bleach the hair above the lip, it is usually still noticeable. Additionally, the chemicals often irritate that sensitive area.

What Body Parts Can She Bleach?

Your daughter can bleach:

- Upper lip
- Forearms
- Stomach

Tools for Bleaching

For the best bleaching, your daughter will need a bleach kit that comes with a cream, a powder, and a spatula.

How to Bleach

1. Mix the cream bleach with the accelerator (a powder that comes with the kit to make the hair bleach faster) in the proportions given in the instructions.
2. Do a patch test.
3. Spread the cream and accelerator mixture over the entire area of dark hair.
4. Leave on for ten minutes.
5. Remove the bleaching mixture by rinsing the bleached area with cool water at the sink. Do not apply moisturizer for twenty-four hours because it could irritate the skin.

Bleaching Tips

- When bleaching forearms, mix only enough for one arm because you can remove the bleach with a spatula from one arm and use it for the other. This is more economical and works perfectly.
- If the mixture feels like it is burning the skin, use less powder the next time.

ELECTROLYSIS AND THERMOLYSIS

Electrolysis has been around since the late 1800s. This method uses an electrical current to remove hair. The electrologist inserts a very fine needle into the hair shaft. The current goes through the needle, destroying the base of the hair. Since the needle stays in the hair shaft and does not go beneath skin tissue, there is neither blood nor much pain. The sensation varies with the individual. The treatments can be uncomfortable.

According to Lucy Peters International, electrolysis uses a current that acts as a catalyst to turn body salt into lye. The hair comes out but may come back. Electrolysis claims to be a permanent method of hair removal. It is not for girls who have not yet gotten their first period. The hormone changes during puberty change hair growth. Any work done before puberty might have to be redone later.

Electrolysis works over the course of several treatments; sessions last anywhere from fifteen minutes to an hour. These treatments can be painful on sensitive areas and you may or may not get permanent results. Electrolysis must be done by a professional, and it can be costly.

Thermolysis is a technology patented by Lucy Peters International that is quite effective in removing hair. As in electrolysis, a needle is inserted into the hair shaft. Unlike electrolysis, however, a concentrated heat rather than an electric current goes through the tip of the probe and damages the hair follicle. To find a thermologist in your area, contact Lucy Peters at www.lucypeters.com.

Both electrolysis and thermolysis hurt on sensitive areas of the body, but for many women, these treatments really work. When your daughter is ready, this is an excellent way to remove unwanted hair, especially in places like the upper lip, between the eyebrows, and the bikini line.

What Most People Don't Know About Electrolysis and Thermolysis

- Hair goes through cycles. A week after shaving, the hair is active and can be removed through electrolysis or thermolysis.
- The eyebrows, upper lip, bikini line, and underarms have the shortest hair cycles. The legs have the longest cycle.
- Typically, facial hair can be removed permanently in six to eight treatments of thermolysis. Electrolysis may take more treatments.
- Electrolysis and thermolysis are costly but efficient. It is more economical to remove hair from the upper lip for a year with electrolysis or thermolysis than pay to have it waxed for the rest of her life.
- Electrolysis and thermolysis *may not* be performed at home. An experienced professional must do it.
- Electrolysis and thermolysis do not leave scars. There may be some irritation, redness, and possibly minor scabbing immediately following electrolysis treatment. These signs go away within a few days. Bruising can sometimes occur with thermolysis, but it goes away.

What follows is a short list of tips to help you find a good electrologist:

- Have a dermatologist recommend someone.
- Check out the electrologist's credentials. If there is a licensing program in your state, make sure this person is licensed to operate in your state.
- The American Electrology Association has chapters in each state. Call them for recommendations. These organizations require an electrologist to complete a course and take tests to certify their skills.

In evaluating an electrologist, here's what you should look for:

- The electrologist *must use* clean, sterilized needles. Watch the person take the needle out of a sealed plastic bag. If the electrologist does not use a clean needle, leave!
- Proper electrolysis uses one of three types of currents: galvanic, thermolysis, or a blend of the two. Anything else is not electrolysis and can be dangerous. Ask your electrologist what method will be used and how the method works.
- Find someone you are comfortable with. This is a highly personal matter, which will have to be done more than once. It is important to like and trust your electrologist.

Finding a good thermologist is a little more difficult. Lucy Peters International (www.lucypeters.com) holds the patent on this technology. So, if you choose this method, you should contact them for a consultation. Unfortunately, the company has only five locations in the United States. If you happen to live near one, this could be a great option. Lucy Peters International will not do thermolysis until a girl has had a stable period each month over the course of a year. At that point, you can bring your daughter in for a consultation, and they will tell you details about how long it will take to remove the hair from a particular area of her body. If you do not live near a Lucy Peters salon, you can call them for a recommendation of a good practitioner in your area.

What Body Parts Can She Have Electrolysis and Thermolysis On?

Your daughter can have these treatments on every part of her body where she has unwanted hair.

Electrolysis and Thermolysis Tips

- It is advisable not to have electrolysis done right before or during menstruation because the body is more sensitive.
- Be extra careful about exposing the treated area to the sun during the course of treatment.

LASER

Laser hair removal has become very popular because it is fast and promises permanent results. However, I would be very careful and cautious about using laser on a young girl, especially if she has dark skin. Because lasers target the melanin in the hair, special lasers must be used on darker skin.

Laser hair removal uses a long-pulse laser to remove the hair. Hair grows in cycles. The laser is able to dislodge the hairs that are in their active growth cycle. Hairs that are in their dormant cycle will need to be treated when they are active. This is why several treatments are necessary to get to all of the follicles in a given area.

I have undergone laser hair removal treatments. It does a good job on dark hairs, but it is ineffective in the removal of fine blonde hairs. There is always a potential it can burn the skin or leave marks that can last up to three months. The treatments are great because they have minimal pain and a large area can be treated quickly.

The FDA does not approve of a laser as a permanent method of hair removal, so I would also take that into consideration before treating your daughter with it. However, if you really want to try it, find a reputable place that specializes in hair removal. Do it to yourself before treating your daughter. Then, make an informed decision.

What Body Parts Can She Have Laser On?

Your daughter can have these treatments on every part of her body where she has unwanted hair.

Laser Tips

- If your daughter has dark skin, be sure to go to a place that specializes in dark skin. There are specific lasers designed for dark skin.
- Find out how much the whole treatment will be before you let her do a session.
- Have the laser done on yourself to make sure you are comfortable letting your daughter do it.
- Go to a reputable dermatologist or salon that you have thoroughly researched.

• Do not laser until a year after the onset of menstruation.

* * *

Good luck during this difficult time! Be the mom you would want to have. If your daughter comes to you for help, be there for her. The old-fashioned reaction of simply saying, "You're too young," will only alienate her and make her feel she is all alone. This can lead to a negative self-image, especially if kids are teasing her at school. If you help your tween with hair removal and show her that her feelings are important to you, she will be grateful for your help—and you may learn a thing or two in the process. Try to help her by doing some of the following activities together.

Bonding Activities

• Take her shopping for a razor. Let her pick out her favorite color and a shaving cream that smells great.
• Order the Completely Bare wax online. It smells great, and you can take turns waxing each other. Pretend your bathroom is a beauty salon and start getting rid of that unwanted, unsightly hair!
• Go to the mall together and have your eyebrows threaded.

CHAPTER 6

Bonding over Puberty & Hygiene

(YES, IT CAN BE DONE!)

As moms, the thought of our daughters going through puberty can be daunting. We have only to think back on when and how we crossed that threshold to realize what's ahead for our own tweens. For instance, I remember the summer when I was nine years old and staying at my grandparents' house. One day I took my shirt off to take a shower. I looked down and saw that my breasts looked like two acorns. I immediately started to blush and wondered how I would hide them—especially in a bathing suit. Around the same time, I noticed an odor under my armpits from sweating. I became insecure about my body, my smell, and just about everything else.

If your daughter is about to or is going through puberty, how you get her through this time in her life is crucial to her self-esteem. I am going to help you teach her to be aware of her body and to develop good hygiene so she will feel confident about herself.

Every healthy female's body undergoes physical changes, starting as young as age eight. By the time they are eleven or twelve, most girls have started developing into young women. However, there are always those late bloomers who don't enter puberty until they are fifteen or sixteen.

During puberty, a girl develops breasts, pubic hair on and around the vulva, and hair under the arms. Perspiration becomes more prevalent, and you and she may notice she has a clear discharge from the vagina about six months prior to menstruation.

And, of course, she gets her monthly period. Suddenly, personal hygiene is a lot more complicated and requires a host of different products. It's time for those embarrassing discussions, which need to be handled with the utmost care. I suggest you initiate these discussions before she goes through puberty. Share your own personal stories about being embarrassed or confused or scared when you saw your body changing. The more humiliating, the better. Make her laugh at you and show her how little you knew at her age. Keep it as matter-of-fact as possible. I always tell my daughter that absolutely nothing she can ask me will ever embarrass me. Becoming a woman is a part of life. She is not the first or last girl in the world to go through it.

It's also important to recognize that some girls are less mature about these things than others. When a preteen or teen is acting silly or indifferent when you bring up the subject, emphasize that she is no longer a little girl and cannot continue with her earlier behaviors, such as walking around in front of her brother without a shirt on. She also has to learn to close her door when she changes clothes.

This would also be a good time to discuss with the male members of your household how important it is for them to be sensitive to the girl in the house who's entering puberty. There is nothing worse for a tween than being self-conscious about her body, only to have her father or brother make some silly comment to further make her want to bury her head under the covers.

So, now let's talk about the specifics of body odors and menstruation, along with good hygiene practices for handling both of these manifestations of puberty. If your daughter is not aware of her changing body, it's time for you to make her aware of smelling clean and fresh. That means everything from her breath down to her toes. If she is developing breasts and has seen some vaginal discharge, it's time to tell her what to expect and how to be prepared for the realities of being a woman.

Body Odors

The tween years are tough in many ways. And as a tween starts to enter puberty, things can get really rough. One of the side effects of puberty and growing up is that certain parts of the body start to smell different. Odors of all sorts may start emanating from your daughter's body, causing new and awful kinds of humiliation. It's your job as her caring mom to help prepare her so that she can avoid as much embarrassment as possible. In the following pages, I've outlined the biggest smelly culprits and how you can help your daughter prevent them.

PERSPIRATION

If your daughter is just entering puberty, you may notice her perspiration is beginning to stain her shirts under the arms and to smell. Odor and wetness can begin for a girl as young as nine years old. That odor is caused when perspiration mixes with the natural bacteria under the arms. When the odors begin, it's time for her to start using antiperspirant or deodorant.

Antiperspirant is absorbed into the pores and blocks perspiration where it starts. Antiperspirants typically contain aluminum, which is thought to have negative long-term effects on the body.

The antiperspirants that keep you the driest, such as the ultradry formulas, contain aluminum.

Deodorant neutralizes the smell of the perspiration mixed with bacteria. While it will control odor, it will not keep her dry.

Every girl and every woman differs when it comes to perspiration. Some have a stronger odor than others, some seem to sweat more than others, and some don't seem to have much of a problem with either. You'll need to work with your daughter to make a decision about what product is best for her needs. Following are some things you might try:

- If she has strong odor and wetness, try a clinical formula like the one made by Secret. To avoid long-term aluminum exposure, your daughter could use a deodorant in the winter and an antiperspirant in the summer months only.
- If your daughter doesn't seem to have much of a problem with wetness, maybe she can use a deodorant on a daily basis and an antiperspirant when it's absolutely necessary, such as big events that may make her nervous or where she will be more active (like presentations, speeches, parties, or dances).
- If you are concerned about the ingredients in antiperspirants or even common deodorants, you might try one of the many natural alternatives available. While not all of them work, some of the national brands have products that work quite well. Keep in mind that while they may help control odor, they won't control wetness. You may have to use a bit of trial

and error to find the one that works best for your daughter. Look for products that contain ammonium alum, baking soda, clay, mineral salts, or tea tree oil or that claim to be long lasting. They typically perform the best.

- If your daughter has sensitive skin, she should use a fragrance-free deodorant or antiperspirant.

Here are some things you should know to control underarm wetness and odor:

- Clear gels and sticks will not keep her as dry as soft solid and solid products will. However, they will not leave white marks on her clothes.
- Always remove underarm hair! The hair traps bacteria, which then mixes with perspiration and causes odor.
- To avoid irritating the skin, wait half an hour after shaving before applying antiperspirant or deodorant.
- Hydrate, hydrate, hydrate. The more hydrated we are, the less concentrated the waste products in our perspiration are. And waste products increase odor.
- Some foods change and affect the intensity of the odor of our perspiration. If your daughter notices that she's smellier some days more than others, ask her to track what she's had to eat to see if the underarm odor is food related.

FEET

Foot odor is a common problem especially among teenagers (see chapter 4, "Bonding over Her Hands & Feet"). To control foot odor, try the following techniques:

- Wash feet daily with soap and water. Dry them well with a clean towel. (Make sure to wash and dry the areas between the toes.)
- Insert charcoal-insulated insoles designed to control odor in your daughter's shoes. It is best for her to alternate shoes so they have time to dry between uses.
- Sprinkle some foot powder in her shoes each morning.
- Wear cotton socks because they absorb moisture better than synthetic fabrics do, and they allow the skin to breathe.
- Wash her sneakers in the washing machine a few times each month to eliminate the odor.

VAGINA

Every woman's vagina has a normal smell that becomes slightly stronger after she exercises or perspires. Your daughter should learn what is normal for her body. If her vagina has an unusually strong, pungent odor, something may be wrong and you must consult a doctor. Here are some helpful hints to keep normal vaginal odor to a minimum:

- Shower daily and immediately after exercising or perspiring excessively.
- Wear 100 percent cotton underwear. It dries quickly and allows skin to breathe.
- Change underwear daily and always bring a fresh pair to change into after exercise, a long car ride, or plane trip.
- Use premoistened vaginal wipes as often as necessary during the hot days of summer and on heavy days of her period.

(Make sure she has a supply of these in the bag or backpack she carries around.) It's like cleaning with soap and water.

- Change tampons and panty-liners every four to six hours during her period. If she uses sanitary napkins, change them once every two hours.

- She should not douche. The doctors I interviewed viewed douching as unnecessary. A douche can sometimes cause vaginal dryness and irritations. Douching can also upset the natural bacteria in the vagina, which can lead to problems such as yeast infections or bacterial vaginosis (see "Common Health Problems" later in this chapter).

BREATH

Bad breath plagues us every morning and throughout the day. No one is immune to it. At night, the mouth becomes dry and traps gases, causing bad breath. Saliva functions to get rid of gases like sulfur. The drier the mouth, the worse the breath. During the day, our mouths get dry due to talking, exercise, illness, and medications like decongestants. To combat bad breath, try these simple measures:

- Teach your tween to brush her teeth and her tongue. The tongue is where most of the gases and bacteria build up. A healthy tongue is pink. If you see white residue, brush it away.

- Get her a travel-size toothbrush and

toothpaste to carry in her backpack at school. Encourage her to brush her teeth after lunch.

- Teach your daughter to floss carefully, especially the back teeth, before she brushes. Food trapped between teeth disintegrates and causes odor.
- Keep the mouth wet by eating foods that contain water and by staying hydrated by drinking water. Fruits and vegetables are a great source of water. My late grandmother swore by eating parsley.
- Avoid foods that contain lots of sulfur, like garlic and onions.
- If she has to burp, tell her to keep her mouth closed and then say "Excuse me." Better yet, have her excuse herself and go to the bathroom to let out the burp.
- Buy a ten pack of mints at the supermarket. Put a pack in each of her bags so she is never stranded without these handy breath fresheners.

If your tween's bad breath seems incurable, talk to your dentist about medical ways to handle this problem.

GAS

Expelling gas can cause embarrassing moments. If your daughter needs to release gas, teach her to politely and quickly excuse herself and go to the bathroom. If she passes gas by accident, she should politely say, "Excuse me," and try to remember that it happens to everybody.

To help control gas, teach her the following tips:

- Tell her to eat slowly and avoid speaking while she chews her food. Eating fast and speaking while eating will make her take in too much air, which gets released on the other end.

- Before an important moment, she should not eat foods that can cause gas, such as high-fiber cereals, fruits, cheese and other dairy products, beans, and soda.
- Going to the bathroom right after eating is helpful. Even if she felt fine at the table, she may realize she has to pass gas once she is in the bathroom.
- Experiment with foods. When foods give her gas, keep a mental note of them. They could be rough on her digestion. Avoid these foods just before an event in which she wants to make a particularly good impression.

Menstruation

When a girl is born, she has thousands of eggs in her body. During puberty, her ovaries release one egg each month. At the same time, the uterus builds up a lining that will support a baby in case the egg becomes fertilized. If the egg is not fertilized, the lining of the uterus wall and the unfertilized egg are released or shed. Blood begins to flow through the cervix and then out of the vagina. While we all know what an inconvenience it can be, getting her period every month means your daughter is a healthy young woman.

Once a woman starts getting periods, they typically come every month until menopause. Periods usually last three to seven days. When she is not having her period, it is perfectly normal to have a thin mucus discharge. It is important for your tween to know and expect this so that she doesn't worry about something being wrong or think she isn't normal. Teach her to keep a calendar and mark the days when she menstruates to learn what is normal for her body. In that way she'll be alert to anything abnormal in her monthly cycle, such as a strange odor, abnormal discharge, or bleeding at the wrong time.

When teaching your daughter about her menstrual cycle and discussing the female anatomy with her, use the correct words. By age nine, she should know the proper names for her body parts, and so should you. (To refresh your memory, consult the Need to Know list on the following page.)

COPING WITH CRAMPS

Cramps are muscle contractions in the uterus. During the three to seven days before and often during their menstrual periods, many girls experience cramping to a greater or lesser degree. By relaxing the stomach muscles, your daughter can lessen the severity of her cramps. The following will help her relieve cramps:

- Take a hot bath or shower.
- Place a heating pad or hot washcloth on her stomach where the cramps are the most severe.
- Dr. Edmund Kaplan, an OB/GYN at Lenox Hill Hospital in New York, recommends taking a pain reliever such as Advil, Motrin, or Midol. If the cramps are so severe your daughter cannot go to school, see a doctor to make sure the pain is not an indication of something more serious.

Need to Know

Cervix—The lower part of the uterus, with an opening that connects the uterus to the vagina.

Clitoris—The most erogenous female sex organ located above the vaginal opening.

Egg (or ovum)—The reproductive cell in a woman.

Fallopian tubes—The pair of tubes that carry the egg from the ovary to the uterus.

Fertilization—The joining of egg and sperm.

Hymen—The fleshy tissue that stretches across part of the vaginal opening.

Labia majora—The outer, fatty folds of the vulva on either side of the opening of the urethra.

Labia minora—The inner, largely connective-tissue folds of the vulva on either side of the opening of the urethra.

Ovaries—The two organs that store eggs in a woman's body.

Ovulation—When an ovary releases an egg.

Sperm—The reproductive cells in men.

Urethra—The tube and opening from which women (and men) urinate.

Uterus (or womb)—The pear-shaped reproductive organ from which women menstruate and where normal pregnancy develops.

Vagina—The passage that connects a woman's outer sex organs with the cervix and uterus.

Vulva—A woman's outer sex organs, including the clitoris, the labia, and the opening of the vagina.

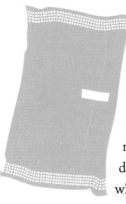

MAXI PADS

Maxi pads come in a variety of shapes and sizes for the different times of a girl's period. They are easy to use because she can just stick them in her underwear. If your daughter sleeps eight hours or more per night, she should use a pad for maximum nighttime protection. Panty-liners are easy to use during the lighter days of her period or on days when she ovulates and has lots of clear discharge.

TAMPONS

I think tampons are great because they allow girls the freedom to do all their normal activities, including swimming and sports, even on the heavy-flow days of their periods. In the summer, she can safely wear a bathing suit without a heavy pad showing through. Just make sure she tucks the string into her bathing suit. I really like OB tampons over all others. They are applicator free, which makes them more compact, and the actual tampon expands to fit the body. Other tampons tend to get longer instead of wider, and the result can be more leaks. While scented tampons are safe to use, I would avoid them because they could irritate your daughter.

In case your daughter asks, yes, virgins *can* use tampons!

To teach her how to insert a tampon safely and comfortably, have her refer to the illustration that comes with the box of tampons, and follow the directions on the next page:

1. Wash hands.
2. Start with the lightest absorbency you can find; these are often labeled a junior or a regular tampon.
3. If she has a tampon with an applicator, have her remove the tampon from the applicator the first time she attempts insertion. (Once she gets used to how it feels to put in a tampon she can experiment with applicators if she does not like using her fingers.)
4. Lubricate the tip of the tampon with a vaginal lubricant or Vaseline Petroleum Jelly. She may only need to do this the first few times she uses a tampon.
5. Have her put one foot up on the edge of the toilet. With her finger at the base of the tampon, have her use the head of the tampon to try to feel around for the opening of the vagina. If she can't find it, looking in a compact mirror held between her legs can be helpful.
6. When she finds the opening, have her push the tampon up as far as it will go with the string hanging outside the vagina. When she no longer feels the tampon, it is in the right place.
7. To remove, she should pull on the string and the whole tampon will come out.

If she has trouble getting the hang of it, take her to her pediatrician (preferably a female for her comfort) and have the pediatrician do it for her the first time.

To avoid bacterial infections such as toxic shock syndrome, always have her use the lowest absorbency necessary and change the tampon every four to six hours, or more frequently if necessary.

A tampon should not be left in for more than eight hours. She can sleep with a tampon if she changes it during the night or sleeps less than eight hours.

AMENORRHEA

Amenorrhea is a fancy name for skipping periods. When a girl first starts menstruating, it's common for her periods to occur irregularly, that is, they can skip over a month rather than come at the same time each month. Amenorrhea can be caused by many common factors, such as stress, weight loss, or lots of exercise (particularly if the tween is an athlete). However, amenorrhea could be an indication of a medical issue, such as pregnancy.

It is essential to seek the help of a health care provider if:

• She has skipped a period when she is usually regular.
• She has skipped more than six periods after menstruation has begun.
• Menstruation has not started by sixteen or seventeen years of age.
• She is sexually active and has missed a period.

PREMENSTRUAL SYNDROME (PMS)

Most girls suffer from some type of PMS. For me, it changes from month to month. Sometimes I cry over a sappy coffee commercial; other months, I've been known to cry for no reason at all. There is no cure for PMS, but there are lots of things you can do to help control the symptoms. The most common symptoms include:

• Bloating, retaining water
• Cramps

- Weight gain of no more than ten pounds
- Painful, swollen breasts
- Headaches
- Crying and feeling depressed
- Mood swings
- Feeling nervous and irritable
- Feeling tired all the time
- Chocolate, salt, and sugar cravings
- Pimples

PMS occurs up to ten days before menstruation begins. Ask your daughter to mark on her calendar when she experiences mood swings, fits of depression, and sweet cravings. After a few months, you and she may notice that, for example, six days before her period she feels moody. By identifying the moods that are PMS related, you will know which ones are nothing more serious than hormone related. Either have your daughter keep away from people during that time, or have her employ some of the following techniques to help her cope with her PMS symptoms.

Mood Swings

When your daughter has mood swings, the whole family may want to head for the hills. Even if she knows her mood swing is related to PMS, the feelings may be so strong that it is difficult to control the tears and outbursts of rage. While the following tips will not get rid of the mood swings completely, they may help with the intensity. She should:

- Avoid caffeine, sweets, and salty foods. Caffeine and sweets intensify mood swings. Salty foods cause water retention.
- Substitute carob for chocolate, sea salt for regular salt, and fatty-acid foods for fatty foods. Avoid processed food, and opt for fish, vegetable, legumes, seeds and nuts, and fruits. Stabilizing her diet will diminish the intensity of the mood swings.
- Dr. Kaplan recommends vitamin-B complex supplements. Vitamin Shoppe carries chewable B-12 vitamins that come in a delicious raspberry flavor. When the body is stressed out, it uses vitamin B, and a low level of vitamin B contributes to mood swings.

Aromatherapy for PMS

Baths are great for PMS symptoms. Mix the following oils together according to the type of PMS symptoms your daughter experiences and add them to a hot bath:

Disagreeableness
>Bergamot: 15 drops
>Geranium: 5 drops
>Nutmeg: 5 drops

Weepiness
>Rose: 9 drops
>Bergamot: 9 drops
>Clary Sage: 12 drops

Fatigue
>Clary Sage: 10 drops
>Grapefruit: 18 drops

TALKING ABOUT THE MENSTRUAL CYCLE AND HOW IT RELATES TO SEX

Talking with your daughter about her period is the ideal time to explain to her how her body works. And yes, you have to talk about sex. You can choose to be vague depending on your daughter's age, but the truth is always best. Explain it all to her using the proper terminology and make her repeat it back to ensure that she has understood all you have said.

Try using the following straightforward explanation or adapting the level of detail to what you're comfortable with and what you sense your daughter is capable of handling at this time.

MONTHLY CYCLE

Her body has approximately a twenty-eight-day cycle. The first day of her period is Day 1. Her next period will come around Day 28. For example, if she gets her period on November 1, she will get her next period around November 29. The length of her cycle will vary from that of her friends due to stress, weight loss, change of environment, and the mere fact that every woman is different. Tell her not to be alarmed if her cycle is twenty-six days and her friend's is thirty-three.

Ovulation

In the middle of the cycle (approximately the fourteenth day), ovulation occurs. An egg is released from the ovary and then moves through the fallopian tube to the uterus.

This is her most fertile time. She will notice a clear discharge on her underwear. (When she wants to get pregnant, this fluid will help the sperm get to the egg.) If the egg is not fertilized, the blood and uterine lining will be released in approximately fourteen days. This is her period.

Fertilization

During sexual intercourse, a man ejaculates sperm into the woman's vagina. Fertilization occurs when the sperm and egg meet. Each ejaculation can contain millions of sperm, yet only one sperm is needed to fertilize an egg. The sperm enters the vagina, swims up through the cervical canal into the uterus, and then enters the fallopian tube where fertilization takes place. When an egg is fertilized, a woman becomes pregnant.

Common Health Problems

As early as age six, girls can get vaginal infections, such as bacterial vaginosis, yeast infections, and urinary tract infections. It is so awful to see your sweet little daughter suffer with this kind of pain or discomfort. Here is a comprehensive list of common vaginal ailments found in young girls regardless of whether they are sexually active. Always see a doctor if she experiences any of these symptoms to make sure she is being treated properly.

BACTERIAL VAGINOSIS

A young girl can get bacterial vaginosis when the normal balance of bacteria in her vagina becomes imbalanced, causing an overgrowth of bacteria. Some of the common discomforts associated with bacterial vaginosis are discharge, odor, vaginal pain, itching, and/or burning. If your daughter has these symptoms, Dr. Kaplan recommends you try a topical cream such as Vagisil. If symptoms persist, see a physician to find out what type of vaginosis your daughter has. Because a yeast infection is the most common type of bacterial vaginosis, I have described it in depth in the paragraphs that follow.

YEAST INFECTION

Candida albicanus is a normal fungus present in the vagina and other parts of the body. Sometimes this fungus grows excessively, which can result in a yeast infection. This type of infection can occur at any age, regardless of whether or not the young woman is sexually active.

Here are some of the common discomforts associated with a yeast infection:

- Thick, white discharge
- Uncomfortable itching

Causes of Yeast Infections
The common causes of a yeast infection include the following:

- Antibiotics
- Walking around in a wet bathing suit and noncotton underwear
- Chemicals and fragrance in bubble baths
- Birth control pills
- Oral sex

- Pregnancy

Treatment

If your daughter is scratching her vulva a lot, especially during the summer months, she should see a doctor for treatment. The over-the-counter vaginal suppositories available to control itching are quite strong and can burn and irritate her internally. I would definitely stay away from them. Instead, use Vagisil topically and have your physician give you a prescription for Diflucan, which clears the infection in three to five days. This option is especially good for younger girls who may not feel comfortable having an applicator inserted in the vagina in order to deliver the medicine.

Prevention

Warm, moist environments are a breeding ground for yeast infections. Fortunately, there are simple steps your daughter can take to avoid providing such an environment. She should:

- Wear 100 percent cotton underwear, because it dries quickly.
- Avoid tight-fitting clothing, especially in the summer.
- Get out of sweaty leotards, bicycle shorts, and wet bathing suits as soon as possible.

URINARY TRACT INFECTION

One out of five women experiences a urinary tract infection (UTI) at some point in her life. Most are easy to cure and not very serious.

Symptoms

Here are some of the common discomforts associated with a UTI:

- A strong urge to urinate
- A burning sensation during urination
- Constant need to urinate, only to find nothing much comes out
- Pressure, sometimes, in the back or abdomen
- Chills, fever, and nausea as well as cloudy urine or a foul odor (these symptoms could indicate a kidney infection)

Causes of UTIs

The common causes of a UTI include the following:

- Wiping back to front instead of front to back exposes the urethra to more bacteria.
- "Holding it in" when the bladder is full and she really has to urinate.
- Sexual intercourse can bring bacteria to the urethra.

Treatment

See a health care provider and have this professional take a urine sample. If your daughter is not menstruating, take her to the pediatrician for treatment. If your daughter is menstruating, Dr. Kaplan recommends treating a UTI with either Uristat (available over-the-counter) or an antibiotic prescribed by her doctor. Her physician may also prescribe Pyridium, which dilates the urethra to minimize the pain and to relieve the burning sensation. This medicine usually takes effect quickly, within a day, but it will turn her urine bright orange, so don't be alarmed.

Prevention

Fortunately, there are simple steps your daughter can take to avoid contracting a UTI. These include the following:

- Drinking cranberry juice daily makes women less likely to experience UTIs. If she already has a UTI, drinking cranberry juice can help to clear up the infection.
- Cleanse the area around the vulva and rectum daily with soap.
- Always wipe from front to back (i.e., vagina to rectum) to avoid spreading bacteria from the rectum to the urethra.

✶ ✶ ✶

I bet you never thought puberty, body odor, and menstruation had anything to do with beauty. They certainly do! A confident woman is a beautiful woman. Teaching your daughter how to care for how pleasant her body smells will give her self-assurance as she matures. Knowing she smells fresh and clean and having the know-how to face the challenges of puberty is something every girl wants. Daily showering is just the tip of the iceberg once womanhood sets in. The key is to keep your conversation about the changes puberty brings sweet and funny rather than critical and judgmental.

If your girl is immature and tunes you out, try tackling just one simple issue at a time. For instance, have her smell her shirt one day after she's been playing and sweating. One whiff of it and she will be interested in deodorant. No one wants to get teased because she smells.

If that goes well, encourage her to become aware of the other smells coming from her body. The menstruation issue is typically the most difficult for moms and daughters alike, so try to approach that with some humor and a good story about you or one of your friends. And while you and I know it is all part of life, it is the biggest deal in the world to her. So, be sensitive, understanding, and most importantly, be cool about it. She will appreciate it more than you can imagine.

Also reinforce how incredible it is that a woman's body has the ability to carry and give birth to and feed a baby. Instead of dwelling on the negatives of being a woman, reinforce the beauty of being a woman and make this time an exciting one for her.

Bonding Activities

- Get some coming-of-age books, like *Are You There God? It's Me, Margaret* by Judy Blume, and suggest that you and your daughter read them together (or separately and discuss it afterward). Girls typically like to read stories about girls going through the same things they are.
- Go shopping for deodorant or antiperspirant together.
- Pick out a light perfume or essential oil together.
- Talk about menstruation and sex and answer all her questions.
- Tell her lots of humiliating stories about yourself so the two of you can laugh at how clueless you were.

CHAPTER 7

Bonding over
Nutrition & Fitness

For a young girl to look and feel her best, she must eat a balanced diet, sleep at least nine hours each night, and get plenty of exercise. As a parent, I often feel as though the world is against me on this one. At birthday parties, pizza and cake are standard fare. Goody bags often contain lots of candy. Snacks consist of chips and soda, and everywhere you turn there is a TV to distract your daughter from what she is putting into her mouth. And, of course, there are the junk food commercials, which are designed to titillate our kids with sugar-filled snacks. Kids are getting more and more homework so they have less time to sleep. And junior varsity and varsity sports have become so competitive that a not-so-great athlete can be too intimidated to participate. So, I completely understand if, as you read this chapter, you ask yourself how you are going to battle all the soda and snack food that seem just fine to other parents, have her get all the hours of sleep in but still get the homework done, and find a way for her to exercise consistently.

As a mom, you should make sure your daughter understands that you want her to eat good wholesome foods because they will keep her healthy. If she wants to look healthy, she actually has to be healthy. She can do every beauty and skincare regimen in the world, but if your daughter is filling herself with processed foods, great skin and good digestion will always be difficult and elusive. This chapter provides basic nutritional knowledge most people do not know, which can help a preteen or teen get through puberty feeling great about herself.

Because girls come in many shapes and sizes, this chapter is not about weight loss; rather, it is about creating a diet and exercise plan that will promote healthy skin, hair, and nails. By making simple changes to your grocery list, adding some vitamin and mineral supplements, and encouraging your daughter to exercise, you can improve her digestion and help her to feel and look great. I also have provided you with ways to help your daughter navigate the school cafeteria as well as food courts and the supermarket.

Shopping for healthy food and trying to figure out which foods do not agree with her are crucial for health and wellness. Remember, one of the ways the body detoxifies is through the skin. If your tween is having skin issues at a young age, food, food sensitivities, pesticides, added hormones, constipation, and even antibiotics could be to blame. All can be upsetting to the normal balance of the body and cause skin breakouts. But the most important part of helping her with a healthy diet is to practice what you preach. If you tell her not to drink soda, you can't drink it either. If you want her to exercise, lead by example. Most importantly, you both need to get your beauty sleep, which is a tall order these days. So, now it's time for you both to eat, sleep, and exercise to be beautiful.

Beauty Starts in Your Kitchen

A healthy diet begins at home. If your daughter's nails are dry and brittle or her skin is covered in blemishes, did you ever think her diet could use a boost? The most common foods we find in supermarkets are often the biggest causes of poor nutrition.

Is your refrigerator packed with sodas and tons of packaged snacks? Is your freezer stocked with frozen prepared dinners and bake-it-yourself pizzas? You can't expect your daughter to look her best if she is constantly eating food filled with hormones and pre-servatives. A great activity for you and your daughter could be the following kitchen makeover. Look at the list of foods in the col-umn labeled Not Great and try to replace them with foods from the Ideal column. Remember to buy organic fruits, vegetables, and dairy whenever possible or at least hormone and antibiotic-free food, which is often less expensive than organic foods. When buy-ing red meat, grass-fed animals are healthier than grain-fed animals. Try to buy meat from free-range chickens. Fish should be wild, not farm raised, and eaten in moderation due to potential mercury content. Milk and cheese should be whole, and eggs should not be separated. The vitamins in milk and eggs are fat soluble, which means the body needs the fats in these foods to properly absorb their vitamins.

Eating for Great Skin

According to Rafael Masiewicz, a certified metabolic typing adviser, skin is a detox organ. Any excess toxins the body can't process through other channels will come out through the skin in the form of breakouts, rashes, and other skin conditions. Con-sequently, it's critical for you to try to minimize environmental toxins such as pesticides, chemicals, artificial colors and flavors, preservatives, and added hormones in your child's food.

Not Great	Ideal
Soda, juice drinks, chocolate milk, sports drinks	Seltzer, water, fresh juices, whole milk, rice milk, almond milk
Canned fruits and vegetables	Fresh fruits and vegetables (If your budget allows it, organics are even better.)
Prepackaged frozen dinners	Fresh hormone- and antibiotic-free meats and fish
Frozen chicken nuggets and fish sticks with many chemical additives	Fresh fish or chicken you bread and fry yourself can be made ahead and frozen. If you do not have time, try to find organic, preservative-free frozen foods.
Packaged presliced cheese with artificial flavors and colors	Fresh cheeses like unsalted mozzarella or cheese sliced for you at the deli counter
Potato chips, pretzels, nachos, cheese-flavored puffs	Unsalted almonds, cashews, pistachios, vegetable chips
Yogurts with high fructose corn syrup, artificial colors, and flavors	Organic plain whole milk yogurt or yogurt with fruit mixed in. For those with dairy allergies, try coconut milk yogurt.
Prepackaged cold cuts bought in the refrigerated section of the supermarket	Freshly sliced cold cuts bought in the deli section of your supermarket
Highly sugared peanut butter with palm oil, or premixed peanut butter and jelly	Unsweetened, all natural peanut and almond butters
Frosted sugary cereals, pancakes from a mix	Sugar-free cereals, oatmeal, porridge, gluten-free cereals (See the section called "Eating for Great Skin" to learn how gluten can cause breakouts if a person has a sensitivity to it.), pancakes made from scratch

Each meal should consist of a protein, a fat, and a carbohydrate. The idea is to keep the blood sugar even to avoid junk food cravings. Junk foods like candy bars and chips can promote breakouts, especially if your daughter has oily skin or you think she could be prone to acne. So, what should she eat to keep her skin looking great?

GOOD PROTEINS

Protein helps to promote healthy growth of hair, skin, and nails. Good proteins are found in meat, chicken, and fish. Eggs are wonderful eaten whole because biotin is found in the egg yolk and protein is in the egg white.

GOOD FATS

Consuming healthy fats such those found in avocados, fresh cheese, chicken, coconut oil, and olive oil will help skin's moisture.

BAD FATS

Rafael recommends not using cooking sprays or eating polyunsaturated fats, hydrogenated oils, or vegetable oils. They can cause inflammation in the body, which can lead to skin irritations.

GOOD CARBS

Fruits and vegetables are loaded with vitamins and minerals, which are great for healthy skin.

BAD CARBS

Many packaged foods are loaded with omega-6 fatty acids. Too much omega-6 (sources include safflower and nut oils, mayonnaise, and margarine, among others) can cause inflammation in the body and lead to skin irritations.

FOODS TO AVOID

The most common ingredients in foods can be the most harmful. If you choose to buy a packaged food, read the ingredients first.

Soy

Soy is high in phytoestrogens, which can aggravate cystic acne. Extra estrogen results in overproduction of oil in the skin, which further clogs pores and results in deep-rooted pimples.

Sugar

Excess sugar in the diet can harm collagen production, which makes skin lose elasticity. It can also make skin appear dull and unhealthy. Consuming highly sugared foods can also lead to insulin problems, which affect hormones and could possibly cause hormone imbalances. Avoid foods that contain high-fructose corn syrup. It is just another word for sugar.

MSG

Monosodium glutamate is a flavor enhancer added to many canned soups, canned vegetables, and packaged meats. It makes foods taste great but can cause terrible headaches, nausea, and even the skin to break out.

Great Snacks

Snacks are important to keep up energy. Great energy will give your daughter the boost to exercise and will bring oxygen to her skin! Have her eat a piece of fruit along with a food that contains a good fat. The fat slows down the metabolism of the fruit sugar. This will keep her feeling fuller longer and her blood sugar more even. Here are some great food combinations to create healthy snacks.

Apple, Pear, or Banana with Peanut Butter or Almond Butter

- Apples and pears are a great source of fiber, which helps the body cleanse itself. They are also loaded with antioxidants, which protect the skin from damage.
- Bananas contain biotin, which is vitamin B-7, an essential for hair, skin, and nail growth.
- Almonds and peanuts are a great source of vitamin E, which helps the skin produce collagen.

Almonds and Blueberries or Raspberries

- Blueberries are high in vitamin C, which is needed to form the protein collagen and to maintain healthy gums and capillaries.
- The oil in the raspberry seed has a natural sun protection factor, which can help protect skin from sun damage.
- The vitamin E from almonds enhances the complexion.

Guacamole or Hummus with Tomatoes, Carrots, or Cucumber slices

- Avocados contain niacin, which is vitamin B-3 and helps

skin retain moisture. Avocados are delicious with sea salt and lemon or eaten in guacamole.

- Hummus is made from chickpeas, which are a great source of protein as well as molybdenum. Molybdenum helps the body detoxify sulfites that are a preservative present in many deli meats and at salad bars in food courts.
- Red tomatoes are rich in the antioxidant lycopene. Lycopene can help neutralize cell-damaging free radicals in the body and thus help prevent skin cell damage.
- Carrots contain vitamin A, which is essential for healthy skin, hair, and nail growth.
- Cucumber juice contains silica, which improves the complexion. Cucumbers—which are essentially water—also hydrate the skin.

Yogurt with Berries and Some Nuts

- The probiotic in yogurt promotes good digestion, which helps promote healthier skin.
- Yogurt is an excellent source of calcium, which can help prevent osteoporosis.
- Many yogurts have extra vitamin D, which is essential to overall wellness.

Dehydrated Coconut (Shredded or in Small Cubes)

- The oil from the coconut improves the complexion.
- Coconut oil contains lauric acid, which helps fight viruses in the body.

Digestion for Beauty

Rafael Masiewicz explained to me that the skin is the body's mirror of health and wellness. You could eat the healthiest foods and supplements out there, but if you are unable to absorb nutrients from these foods, your body will just cast them off as expensive waste products. Many girls have food sensitivities that can cause a variety of skin reactions. I am not referring to life-threatening food allergies but rather to more subtle reactions such as psoriasis, dermatitis, eczema, and acne. The most common food sensitivities are to gluten, dairy, and eggs. Remember, the skin is a detoxification organ. So if you or your daughter notices any of the skin conditions just mentioned, as well as bloating in the stomach, you may want to experiment with your diets.

My daughter and I are a perfect case study. We always had red bumps on the back of our arms. In fact, every woman in my family has them. My daughter also had bloating in her stomach and eczema behind her ears. Rafael suggested we remove the gluten and dairy from our diets. At first, we just removed the gluten. After thirty days the red bumps were gone. But the eczema and bloating still remained for my daughter. So, I experimented with the dairy. Sure enough, removing the dairy got rid of the eczema. Then I had my daughter tested for food allergies. It turned out she had an acute sensitivity to the caseins in dairy products.

Even though each case is different, I strongly encourage you to look at your daughter's skin as an indicator of what may be going on in her body. If she has skin conditions, play with her diet and explain to her that you think she might have a food sensitivity that needs to be addressed. Above all, take some simple steps in adjusting her diet before you take more severe actions such as using acne medications or harsh topical creams, which could potentially perpetuate the problem they are supposed to be treating.

Hydrate, Hydrate, Hydrate

Rafael Masiewicz recommends drinking water filtered with a reverse osmosis filter or bottled spring water. If you can find water in glass bottles it is preferable; that's because some plastic bottles contain bisphenol-a, or BPA. This toxic chemical is also an estrogen mimicker and can lead to acne. So, if your daughter has acne, try to limit her exposure to plastics that may leach BPA into products she may be ingesting.

Remember: Hydrating means *water*, not juices, sports drinks, sodas, diet sodas, or sugar-flavored waters. I know this is tough for kids, especially when they are at a friend's house or a party. But try to explain to her why sodas and sports drinks are bad for her and never keep them in the house or drink them in front of her. If it's really a problem getting her to drink plain water, make your own lemonade or iced tea.

Pink Lemonade

1. Squeeze the juice of four large lemons and pour it into the pitcher.

2. Liquefy a box of strawberries or raspberries in the blender.
3. Mix the lemon juice and liquefied berries in the pitcher. Add water and ice to fill the pitcher.

Iced Tea
1. Add two decaffeinated tea bags to a pitcher of boiling water.
2. Let steep for ten minutes. Refrigerate.
3. Drink with a squirt of lemon and lots of ice.

Though I suggest unsweetened tea, you could always make it with a little honey or agave to make it more appealing.

Nutritional Supplements

If your daughter is able to swallow a vitamin, consider supplementing her diet with vitamins and minerals to make sure she is getting all the nutrients that she needs as she grows. Ideally, you should use whole food vitamins and minerals, which are easier on

the stomach. (Several chewable vitamins are available too if she doesn't like to swallow pills.) Be aware, however, that even though the kids love the gummy-type vitamins, many of them are just a slightly healthier version of gummy bear candy. They often do not contain enough of the vitamin in each dose. Ideally, vitamins should come from foods, of course, but Rafael Masiewicz recommends you look for vitamin and mineral supplements that contain the following for great hair, skin, and nails:

- Vitamin A: Maintains and repairs skin cells (if your daughter's skin is flaky, she could be deficient in vitamin A)
- Vitamin E: Supports collagen production
- Copper and zinc: Good for acne and help boost elastin
- Vitamin C: Reduces premature aging
- Omega-3: Helps combat dry skin

Keeping Up the Beauty Diet at School

Cafeterias in our schools are more about feeding kids economically than nutritionally. I know it is tough to control what she is putting into her mouth when you aren't there. Nevertheless, you can talk about it abstractly and share with her what you're learning about nutrition—from this book and any other sources. It may seem like she is tuning you out, but I bet she will remember some of the following tips the next time she is standing in the cafeteria line with her tray (these tips also apply to a food court in a mall or a buffet at a restaurant):

- Do not go back for seconds! She should get everything she wants the first time she goes through the line. If she sticks to this, she will not get in the habit of going back for more.
- Avoid the lunch specials. The specials are prepared in bulk with little attention paid to the content of the sauces. They are also highly salted and sugared to mask the lack of flavor.
- Salad bars can be the devil in disguise. Go to the salad bar for vegetables, beans, fruits, and vegetables. Substitute oil and vinegar for the premade ranch or blue cheese dressing

and avoid the processed cheeses and croutons. Often, pre-made dressings contain "natural flavors"—another way of saying MSG.

- Only drink water. Diet soda and fruit drinks have no nutritional value. Stick to mineral waters.
- Coffee is a killer. So, you think a cappuccino is just coffee? How about the two packages of sugar everyone dumps into the coffee? If coffee is a part of your daughter's life, she should get used to it unsweetened.
- Fro-Yo as a meal substitute is a myth. Frozen yogurt is a dessert to eat instead of ice cream. It is not a healthy lunch, nor is it slimming. It tastes so good because it is full of sugar. Top it with granola, sprinkles, honey, and chocolate chips, and you have a high-glycemic dessert, not a well-balanced lunch.
- Choose tea with lemon. Drinking herbal or green tea with lemon after meals helps digestion.
- Eat carbs last! Tell your daughter to find a protein like chicken, fish, or beans among the cafeteria offerings, and mix it with a fat like cheese, olive oil, or nuts before she eats anything else. She will find herself eating fewer carbs because she has already filled up on the protein and good fat.
- Desserts are a disaster. The more dessert you eat, the more you want. Dessert needs to be tea and fruit not cake and ice cream.

Exercise

Vegging in front of the TV never brought out the beauty in anyone. In fact, what everybody needs is lots and lots of exercise to bring oxygen to the skin and to promote healthy blood flow. When your daughter exercises, her body releases toxins while she sweats, which will keep her spirits high and make her look and feel her best. If you live in a city, it is harder to get kids outside, so you need a regimen of after school activities to keep her body active and moving daily. If your daughter's school does not offer after school sports, consider your local Y. They usually have a wide variety of activities for kids. And don't forget your local parks. Get your daughter on those jungle gyms as much as possible. They are specifically designed for kids to have fun while burning off all that energy. If you are working full time, see if she can go to the park with other caregivers during the week and you can take the kids on the weekends.

If you live in the suburbs, get her a bike to ride instead of driving her everywhere. Make sure she gets plenty of long walks and jungle gym time or have her join a team at school. It does not matter what kind of exercise or sport she does. All that counts is that she is active and getting her blood pumping daily. I guarantee she will look and feel healthier.

CREATING AN EXERCISE REGIMEN

Great skin and a healthy body are two wonderful benefits of exercise. Get familiar with the following list to learn how to make exercise effective and fun so your tween or teen does it regularly.

Ten Inspirations for Exercise

1. She should work out every day, playing and doing something she enjoys.

2. Exercise should include a minimum of fifteen minutes of aerobic activity (but not on a treadmill), which raises the heart rate. Girls should be doing fun things like climbing, jumping rope, swimming, cheerleading, and participating on sports teams.

3. If your daughter is self-conscious about not being able to keep up with her friends, buy her a hip-hop CD or DVD so she can dance to the music.

4. Have her do something unusual like boxing, dancing, yoga, or mountain biking. If she is concentrating on mastering a sport, she will not be checking her watch every ten minutes.

5. Buy a jump rope and have her double Dutch with friends.

6. The Wii makes Dance Revolution which is a fun workout she can do at home!

7. Exercise with her. I love to surf, so I take my daughter with me when I go. She loves spending time with me and feels so cool hanging out with all the surfers.

8. Make exercise a part of your whole family's life. Plan trips around activities such as hiking, mountain biking, skiing, or swimming.

9. If you have a dog, have her run with the dog

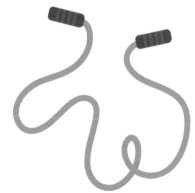

around your block. They will both come back refreshed and—hopefully—a little tired.

10. After she exercises, make home like a spa. Get her favorite products, dry and style her hair, and apply body lotion.

EMPHASIZE HER BEAUTY

Do not criticize your daughter's weight or allow anyone in your household to do so. Her self-esteem is in a fragile place during the pubescent years. Combine that with a changing body and you can have a very insecure young girl who is sensitive to even the slightest criticism of her appearance. No matter what her body type, emphasize health and wellness over being thin. If she tries a new activity, encourage her by telling her how great she looks as a result of the new activity. If you find something she is good at, encourage her to pursue that activity and persevere when it gets challenging.

TALK TO HER

Talk to your special girl each night about her feelings and tell her it's okay to cry. Crying releases feelings and allows her to let go of her pain and release it from her body. The red eyes are temporary but the therapeutic benefits of a good cry are long lasting. Help her by being sensitive to the feelings she has and listen to her when she tells you how she feels. Sometimes, girls overeat because they are unhappy and take comfort in that pint of ice cream. If she has an outlet to let out her feelings and frustrations, she might not need that box of cookies.

* * *

Fitness and good nutrition are a way of life. Most people find life-style changes easier if they make those changes with a partner. Take this opportunity to do something for yourself as well as your daughter. Change your diet and the foods you buy for your family. Start by keeping your refrigerator stocked with healthy food, not junk. Make a list with your daughter and take her shopping. Challenge her to find healthy recipes you can create together. Learn more about nutrition with great books like the *Metabolic Typing Diet* (available at http://www.metabolictyping.com). Most importantly, keep it simple. Do not count calories or complicate your life with difficult recipes you don't have time to cook. Simple whole foods are the key to good nutrition; a healthy body; and beautiful hair, skin, and nails.

Bonding Activities

- Find a great recipe and have your daughter write down all the ingredients you will need. Take her shopping and have her help you prepare the new recipe.
- Go through the pantry with your daughter and get rid of all the junk food.
- Go to William Sonoma or your local bookstore and pick out a new healthy cookbook. They have great books with healthy recipes kids can make. Have your daughter pick out a recipe for something she would like to make and do it together.
- Take her for a bike ride, a hike in the park, or a swim in your local pool.
- Try a new activity together. I decided I wanted to learn to surf. On a day when the waves were calm, we took a surfing

lesson together. It was so much fun and the best part was we did it together!

- Pick out some dance games for the Wii and challenge your daughter to a dance off. It's so much fun, you won't even feel like you are exercising.
- Take her and her friends to your local playground before seeing a movie.
- After she exercises, treat her to an at-home spa experience with all her favorite products.
- Take her to the farmer's market and get to know your local farmers. You are teaching her to support her community while enjoying local farm fresh produce. You are also getting more vitamins from your fruits and vegetables because local foods are picked when they are riper and thus have more of the vitamin content than the foods flown in from overseas, which were picked when green.
- Visit a local farm so she learns that fruit does not come from the supermarket.
- Buy some seeds and plant fruits and vegetables in your backyard or in a community garden.

CHAPTER 8

Bonding over Aromatherapy to Feel Beautiful

Our sense of smell is one of the most powerful human senses. When you first smell a new scent, you link it to an event, a person, a thing, or a moment. Aromas can trigger positive thoughts or agitate us because of such associations. During this time of change in your daughter's life, you can tap into this strength by using aromatherapy to calm, soothe, or invigorate her.

Have you ever walked into a person's house and it smelled like fresh flowers? All of a sudden, an ordinary home felt beautiful. If your daughter comes home from school feeling a little blue, walking into her room to find it smelling of lavender will surely brighten her spirits. By adding sachets to her drawers and diffusing scented oils into her room, you can turn her environment into one of comfort and beauty.

This chapter gives you some fun ideas to make her home environment as beautiful as she is. You will learn to make sachets for her drawers, customized room sprays for her bedroom, and flower arrangements to brighten up your home. It is a creative activity you can do together or with her friends. I have also included ways to incorporate aromatherapy into your lives. If you are noticing obstinate, moody behavior from your daughter, there are some great oils you can add to a bath or a wet washcloth to help her calm some of those hormonal mood swings. If she needs to stay up late to study, peppermint oil is a better alternative to caffeine consumption. There are so many different companies making essential oils today. You can purchase these oils at specialty supermarkets, health food stores, and plenty of websites. I encourage you to buy a few basic oils and try some of the ideas in this chapter.

Enjoy your journey into aromatherapy. My daughter absolutely loves it!

Shopping List

Note: The Aveda Institute in New York City specializes in aromatherapy. They provided me with the definitions on the following page and many of the techniques found in this chapter.

What to Make with Essential Oils

The fun part of using essential oils is that you can make whatever products you want. All you need are the basics on the shopping list and you can make room fresheners, sachets for drawers and closets, and oil mixtures for your personal use. And it's a fun activity to do on a rainy day.

Kim Nicole Hochstadt, aromatherapist at Mukta Jala in New York City, recommends using essential oils in a bath, in a foot soak, mixed with unscented shower gels or shampoo (Aveda Shampure is fragrance-free and designed to mix with your favorite oils), or with a diffuser. I have outlined a few recipes here, but if you really enjoy this activity, pick up a book on essential oils. Kim warns that some oils, such as peppermint, for example, are stronger than

Need to Know

Aromatherapy—The belief that aromatic essences of plants and flowers have therapeutic benefits. Benefits can be physiological, psychological, and cosmetic.

Aromatic essence—Through evaporation and distillation, the absolute essence of the botanical matter is extracted in liquid form, allowing the natural properties to be obtained at their ultimate level of purity and potency.

Absolute essence—The plant's life force is a combination of properties known as the absolute essence.

Aromatic oil—Oil made up of pure plant essences. Aromatic oils have many uses, as you will see in this chapter. They can be bought in many supermarkets and health food stores or ordered online.

Diffuser—A diffuser has two levels. A candle goes in the bottom chamber, while the top holds water mixed with aromatic oils. The candle keeps the water and the oil hot allowing the molecules to diffuse into the air for a long period of time. If you can't find a diffuser, add your oils to a bowl of boiling water.

Spritz bottles—Keep your mixtures of aromatic oils and water in plastic spritz bottles, which allows you to spray the mixture wherever you like.

Wicker baskets—Wicker baskets are pretty and practical for holding dried flowers or scented wooden fruits.

others, such as lavender. So you must be sure to dilute them with another oil. You can use baby oil, coconut oil, or olive oil for that purpose.

Take your daughter to a store that sells essential oils and have her choose a few of her favorites. Choose some for yourself, too. At the top of your list should be these must-have oils that Kim recommends:

- Peppermint: For energy and digestion. Peppermint should never touch the eye or be put directly on the skin because it can burn. If it gets in the eye, rub off with any type of oil in your kitchen or baby oil just not water. Oil removes oil. Water spreads the oil.
- Lavender: To calm down and get a good night's sleep. It is very gentle and can be used on any skin type.
- Grapefruit, lemon, or tangerine: For freshness and to control odors. Lemon also kills germs and is wonderful to use in the room when your daughter is sick.

ROOM, SHEET, AND BATHROOM SPRAY

You and your daughter can make your own special spray for the bedroom, for sheets, and to keep the bathroom smelling beautiful. Mix six or seven drops of aromatic oil with water or rose water in a spritz bottle. Spray it in the closet to keep clothes smelling sweet, onto sheets just before going to bed, and in the bathtub or shower. If you are going to spray an essential oil on the sheets, use something calming like lavender or chamomile.

SACHETS

You can buy sachets, but I like to make them because it's less expensive, and it's a nice project. Sachets can be put under pillows, in closets, or hung on the wall to freshen any room.

1. Wrap a fistful of dried flower heads or potpourri in a breathable fabric. An old handkerchief is ideal. Or just use some lace, gauze, silk, cotton, or muslin.
2. Wrap the package with string or ribbon.
3. For added aroma, pour some aromatic oil onto the sachet and place it where you like.

Essential Oils to Fit the Occasion

I am a big believer in aromatherapy to help wake up, to improve studying and memorization, to help stay up late, to boost self-confidence, and to quiet the mind when trying to fall asleep. You can use a spray bottle or diffuse aromatic oils that correspond to your tween's moods or the effect you are trying to achieve. If you don't have a diffuser, add a few drops of oil to an open pot of boiling water. Here are some fun potions you can make together.

MORNING WAKE-UP

The best oils to use in waking up your sleepyhead are

- Peppermint
- Eucalyptus
- Active Composition by Aveda

If your daughter struggles to get out of bed in the morning and to keep her eyes open at the breakfast table, this may be just the thing you need. Fill a spray bottle with water. Add four drops of peppermint oil and/or eucalyptus oil or Active Composition. Spray it around her room, near her bed, but be careful not to get too close to her eyes. Or keep these oils in a diffuser by her bed and light the diffuser when you go in to wake her.

STUDYING AND MEMORIZING

Kim recommends the following oils to promote concentration:

> Lemon
> Jasmine
> Lavender

While she is studying, diffuse one of these oils into the air.

Other oils can help people memorize and retain information faster and more effectively. Try the following blend when she is studying:

> Basil: 9 drops
> Lavender: 8 drops
> Rosemary: 4 drops
> Grapefruit: 10 drops

Mix together this potion, and diffuse five drops into the room.

STAYING UP LATE

The best oils to use in helping your daughter occasionally stay up late are:

Peppermint
Rosemary
Camphor
Eucalyptus
Lemon
Black Pepper

By late middle school, cramming for tests can become a way of life. Why study all semester when you can pull a couple of late-night cram sessions, right? If this sounds like your daughter, I have the perfect, natural way to help her stay awake because caffeine is not a good way to do it.

Place a diffuser or bowl of boiling water on a hard surface near the workspace, but far enough away where it won't get knocked over. Add one of the stay-up-late oils to the water and let it diffuse. The stimulating aroma will get her through even the toughest paper or review for a major test.

CONFIDENCE BOOSTERS

Some essential oils, detected subconsciously, can help boost your daughter's self-confidence:

Lemon
Neroli
Grapefruit
Coriander

Orange
Verbena
Bergamot
Melissa

Diffuse a few drops of any confidence booster oil or put three drops on a handkerchief and have her breathe in the aroma. Again, be sure she avoids her eyes.

Kim suggests you add essential oils to any type of oil and mix them together. Then add the mixture to bath water. The oil will dilute the essential oils and help it mix into the water.

Making your daughter's world smell good will make her feel good. The way her clothes and room smells is as important as how she looks and smells. Imagine meeting a person who looks great but had clothes that reeked of mothballs. It definitely takes away from her overall appearance. If your daughter feels confident in the way she smells and happy in the aroma of her surroundings, she will feel better in general.

SLEEPY TIME
The best oils to use in helping your daughter fall asleep are calming oils such as these:

Lavender
Chamomile
Sandalwood
Geranium
Lemon
Jasmine
Rose

In the tween years, anxiety can start to ramp up. Add in hormonal changes and you've got a good recipe for insomnia. The best way for your tween to relax if insomnia is becoming a problem is to take a hot bath with calming oils before bed, diffuse a calming oil, or better yet, rub her feet with oils.

Other ways to use essential oils to improve sleep include:

* Adding a calming oil or chamomile tea bag to a diffuser or bowl of bowling water. Allow the aroma to permeate the room.
* Making your daughter a cup of chamomile tea to relax and comfort her.
* Putting calming oil in her hair and rubbing it into her scalp. Comb through her hair with a large paddle brush. (The Aveda wooden paddle brush is specifically designed for this.) After fifteen minutes, wash out the oil.
* Spritzing a mixture of lavender oil and water onto her bed linens to make them smell fresh and clean and to help calm her.

Flower Arrangements

Making beautifully scented flower arrangements can be a wonderful creative activity. If you have a garden, be sure to plant some sweet-smelling roses, white lilies, sweet peas, and other flowers you and your daughter like. If you do not have a garden, ask your local florist what day they receive fresh flowers. Often you can go the day before and get discounted flowers.

Once you choose the flowers you like, cut them at a slant and put them in a vase with water and a little powdered plant food. Remember, anything can be a vase—a cup, a pitcher, or even a teapot. Have your daughter arrange the flowers as she likes them. As long as she is not allergic, set them next to her bed for a better night's sleep.

* * *

Once you start experimenting with aromatherapy, it will truly become a way of life. In my home, we have about ten different oils we like. When my daughter takes a bath, she chooses her favorite oil and we add it to her bath or her shampoo. Her friends love to come over, too, to make their own customized shampoos and room sprays.

Incorporating aromatherapy in your girl's day to help her wake up, study, and relax and stay calm is a wonderful way to handle stress and a fun activity for you both to share. Start with a few of your favorite oils and see where the experience takes you.

Bonding Activities

- Make a special room spray for her room and bed linens.
- Draw her a bath with all her favorite essential oils.
- Add her favorite oils to an unscented shampoo or body wash.
- Wake her up with a warm washcloth scented with peppermint.
- Take her to the health food store and let her pick out three of her favorite essential oils.
- Make sachets for her closet and dresser drawers.
- Give homemade room sprays or sachets you and your daughter make together as gifts.
- Make sachets and room sprays and sell them to raise money for your favorite cause.

CHAPTER 9

Bonding over Getting Her Ready to Be Away from Home

If your daughter is going away to summer camp, on a trip out of state or abroad, on a Girl Scout camping trip, or simply to a friend's house for the weekend, this chapter will offer you some great tips for packing everything she will need. Especially if you have an older tween who's going to be away from home for a while (a week or more), many changes could occur, and you won't be right there to help or advise her. So prepare her ahead of time. What should she do if she gets her first period? Maybe she will want to shave her legs for the first time because other girls are doing it. Or she might have to shower communally and not know what to expect. Whatever it may be, talk about it ahead of time so she is prepared for virtually any situation that might arise.

When my niece went to camp for the first time, she was very nervous about being away from home, so I made her a checklist of all of the things she would need. She took the checklist when she and her mom went shopping, and the list helped her to get organized and to feel more in control about the summer ahead. It also gave her a chance to talk with her mom and me about all of the experiences she could expect. She was eleven at the time, so her mom took the opportunity to explain what she should do if she got her period. To help you get prepared, I have made checklists for sleep-away camp, for going out of state or abroad, and for a camping trip.

It's not easy sending your girl off on her own, but if she is confident that she has what she needs, you both will feel better about her time away from home.

Sleep-Away Camp

If your daughter is going to be away for a week or more at a summer camp, do not assume she can just pick up what she needs wherever she is. Buy her toiletries in your hometown and pack them. Most camps do not provide much more than first aid products.

Before packing, take your daughter to the drugstore or supermarket and have her run her hands from the top of her head down over her face and down the rest of her body. This will remind both you and her to buy the things she needs for each part of her body. Her hands on her head will remind you to buy shampoo and conditioner. Her hands on her face will remind you to buy sunscreen, cleanser, lip balm, etc. This technique can help, but the "Packing Checklist for Long Trips" on the following page (together with the tips in the next section that apply to your daughter's stay) will make sure you cover all of the bases.

Packing Checklist for Long Trips

Hair

- ☐ Shampoo, conditioner, detangling spray
- ☐ Comb, brush, curlers
- ☐ Bobby pins and barrettes
- ☐ Elastic bands
- ☐ Headbands
- ☐ Hair dryer
- ☐ Flat iron

Face

- ☐ Tweezers for brows
- ☐ Makeup and lip moisturizer/balm
- ☐ Depilatory for hair above the lip
- ☐ Liquid facial cleanser
- ☐ Pimple cream
- ☐ Moisturizer with SPF 15–30
- ☐ Travel-size toothbrush and toothpaste
- ☐ Dental floss
- ☐ Cotton from a roll of unsterilized cotton—one piece for each day of the trip
- ☐ Makeup remover toilettes (I love the ones by Neutrogena)
- ☐ Tissue packets

Nails and Body

- ☐ Nail file and clippers
- ☐ Nail polish and remover pads
- ☐ Antiperspirant/deodorant
- ☐ Sunscreen with an SPF of at least 30
- ☐ Razor, razor blades, and shaving cream
- ☐ Baby oil or body lotion
- ☐ Tampons, pads, panty-liners
- ☐ Baby powder
- ☐ Liquid body wash
- ☐ Corn pads, moleskin, and bandages (walking a lot can cause blisters)
- ☐ Antifungal spray for athlete's foot
- ☐ Flip-flops (to wear in communal showers)

First Aid and Medicine

- ☐ Lotion for bug bites and bee stings
- ☐ Insect repellent (DEET free)
- ☐ Band-Aids
- ☐ Cotton swabs

To Be Provided to the Adult Supervisor

- ☐ Pain reliever for headaches, cramps, and fever
- ☐ Cold remedies that relieve symptoms without drowsiness
- ☐ Small bottle of antiseptic
- ☐ Full supply of prescription medication and copy of prescription for refills if necessary
- ☐ Yeast infection and bladder infection remedies, if common

Going Out of State or Abroad

If your older tween will be away for a month and is already shaving or waxing, have her wax her legs, underarms, upper lip, eyebrows, and bikini line so she can go the majority of the trip without needing to shave. But pack a razor and shaving cream in case any hair grows back before she returns home.

If she's traveling abroad, her hair dryer must have alternate settings for different types of currents or outlets. Equally important is for her to have brought her own toiletries, because they are much more expensive overseas, and it is always a challenge to find exactly the same products you have at home.

Instead of large bottles of shampoo, use travel-size bottles. She can discard each empty bottle when she uses up the product. This is also great if she will be taking weekend trips from a central location.

Do not forget a small, double-sided magnifying mirror for putting on makeup, tweezing eyebrows, etc.

Give all prescribed medicine to the adult responsible for your daughter to ensure that she takes it properly and responsibly.

If your daughter is prone to yeast or bladder infections, she knows what they feel like. It is always preferable she see a doctor if she detects the symptoms; if she gets a yeast infection in a foreign country, however, you don't want her trying to explain it in a foreign language to a pharmacist. See her physician before your daughter leaves and get four doses of yeast infection and bladder infection medicine. Also pack some Vagisil for vaginal itch. Give this to the adult responsible for her in case she needs it. Also, make sure to tell your daughter to change her underwear at least once during a long plane trip or train ride. Sitting in the same underwear for an extended period of time does not allow moisture on the panties to dry. Pack her a fresh pair of cotton underwear in a ziplock plastic bag.

Camping

When going camping and backpacking, choose only the most important toiletries from the packing list shown previously. It is important to choose enviro-safe products whenever possible. The following items are ideal both for personal hygiene and for protecting the environment.

All-purpose soap. Camping stores and health food stores sell soaps that can be used as a shampoo, detergent, and even toothpaste. These soaps are environmentally safe and will not pollute streams if you bathe with them. Try any of Dr. Bronner's Magic Soaps.

Detangling spray is great for long hair because it doesn't have to be rinsed out but still keeps hair from getting knotted.

Tea tree oil is a natural antiseptic. A tiny bottle will provide relief for toothaches, canker sores, and cold sores. It may also be used to dry pimples.

OB applicator-free tampons are compact to carry and create little waste since there is no elaborate packaging or applicator.

Have her bring ziplock plastic bags and a resealable plastic container. Tell her to place used tampons in the ziplock bag and then place the bag in the airtight container. This will keep her refuse away from clothes until she reaches civilization.

Maxi pads should be ultrathin because they are smaller and more compact.

Premoistened vaginal wipes are an alternative to toilet paper. They are compact and more hygienic than toilet paper. They can also be discarded into the plastic container.

* * *

Now that you have your checklists, it is time to go shopping and get everything your traveling daughter will need. Be enthusiastic about her time away even if you are desperate to keep her home. If she feels you are hesitant about her leaving, it will be harder for her to leave.

A week before she leaves, devote some time just to her. In addition to shopping and packing her bags together, go to a salon if you can and have her hair cut, if your budget allows, get her a Brazilian Blowout if she has frizzy unmanageable hair, do manicures and pedicures together, maybe see a movie, or go out to lunch. It will be fun for both of you and a great way to send her off!

Bonding Activities

- Shop for toiletries.
- Get your hair cut together.
- Give her a manicure and pedicure.
- Wax or thread all the areas that need to be done.
- Take photos of your girls' day and make a digital album.
- Shop for pretty stationery so she will write you letters.
- Watch a fun movie about summer camp or a young girl going on a trip.
- Go to your local bookstore to pick out a great book and a diary.

Journal

Afterword

I sincerely hope *Bonding over Beauty* has given you a perspective you may not have considered previously. Girls are reaching puberty younger than ever before. Combine this fact with the imagery about female beauty that girls see on television, in movies, in magazines, and on the Internet, and you have the fixings for a precocious tween who is slamming doors and saying "you are clueless" before she has given up her blankey and stuffed animals. It is oftentimes confusing and frustrating for mothers to know how to react to their daughters in those moments. That's why I wrote *Bonding over Beauty*. I hope you keep a copy on the shelf to reference when you need a way to engage your daughter and show her you aren't "clueless"—especially about all the beauty issues that will come up.

Please keep in mind that this book is not about making your daughter "beautiful" or turning her into a beauty queen. Rather, it is about helping her deal with the joys and struggles all girls face as they grow into womanhood. I want your daughter to consider you the best resource to help her handle the beauty and hygiene issues that come with adolescence and puberty. I also want you to seem like the "coolest" mom in the world to her. The mom who knows how to make masks for at-home facials and how to style her hair is as much fun as the mom who bakes great brownies. So, try some of the bonding activities with your girl and just let her talk about whatever is on her mind. During these special times you can find out a lot about her thoughts and feelings—and share some of your own.

Bonding over Beauty is also an opportunity for you to think about yourself and reflect on what you wish your mother had taught you. How could your mom have made you trust in her more? Did she tell you all you needed to know about menstruation before it happened? If she did, did you feel later on you could talk to her when you had a problem with a boy? Perhaps you were more of a tomboy in your girlhood and now you're raising a "girlie girl" and you feel out of your element with all her sparkles and glitter. Whatever your personal situation is, this book can help you look at your daughter for who she is and help her be her own person rather than a mini version of you.

One of my favorite parts about researching this book was asking my daughter's advice on how I should wear my hair and makeup. She looked at me from a fresh, young perspective and helped me update my look, which made her feel great and even more connected to me. So, be open-minded. If you don't wear lipstick, try it with her. If you think all of this talk about hair and nails and makeup and pedicures is just for older girls, think again. Don't miss your chance to "bond over beauty" with your daughter no matter what her age. I promise you this: the time you invest will be a special experience she—and you—will never forget.

Index

About the Author

Erika Katz was initiated into the beauty industry at the age of three months, when she appeared with her father on the front cover of *Babytalk* magazine. By the age of thirteen, she had appeared in more than a hundred television commercials and several Hollywood and television films, had been photographed by Richard Avedon, and had modeled for numerous catalogs and national magazines.

After graduating from Dartmouth College with degrees in French and psychology, Erika interned in the beauty department at *Seventeen* magazine. Using her experience at *Seventeen*, cosmetology classes, and lessons learned through her extensive work in television and modeling, she created a beauty guide that served as the foundation for *Bonding over Beauty*.

Erika lives in New York City with her husband and two children. She is involved with NYC-Parents in Action and blogs for her website www.bonding overbeauty.com.